COLLINS GEM
CATS

*a mine of information*

COLLINS GEM
A...

D1132499

COLLINS GEM
HORSES
& PONIES

*a mine of information*

COLLINS GEM
INSECTS

*a mine of information*

COLLINS GEM
KINGS &
QUEENS

*a mine of information*

COLLINS GEM
MUSHROOMS
& TOADSTOOLS

*a mine of information*

COLLINS GEM
SNAKES

*a mine of information*

COLLINS GEM
SPIDERS

*a mine of information*

COLLINS GEM
STRESS
Survival Guide

*a mine of information*

COLLINS GEM
TAROT

*a mine of information*

COLLINS GEM
WINE
Guide

*a mine of information*

COLLINS GEM
WORLD
atlas

*a mine of information*

COLLINS GEM
YOGA

*a mine of information*

COLLINS GEM
ZODIAC
Types

*a mine of information*

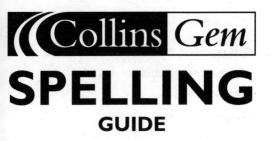

# SPELLING
## GUIDE

CollinsGem

*An Imprint of* HarperCollins*Publishers*

First published 1997

First published in this format 2000
**First reprinted 2001**

© HarperCollins Publishers 1997

ISBN 0-00-710200-3

All rights reserved

Collins Gem® is a registered trademark of
HarperCollins Publishers Limited

The HarperCollins website address is
www.**fire**and**water**.com

10 9 8 7 6 5 4 3 2

A catalogue record for this book is available
from the British Library.

**Corpus Acknowledgements**
We would like to thank those authors and
publishers who kindly gave permission for
copyright material to be used in the Bank of
English. We would also like to thank Times
Newspapers Ltd for providing valuable data.

Typeset by Davidson Pre-Press, Glasgow

Printed in Italy by Amadeus S.p.A

**CONTENTS**

## EDITORIAL STAFF

*Publishing Manager*
Diana Treffry

*Managing Editor*
Sheila Ferguson

*Editors*
**Mary O'Neill**

Ian Brookes        Lorna Gilmour
Andrew Holmes    Elspeth Summers

*Computing Staff*
Jane Creevy
Robert McMillan

### *Acknowledgement*

The editors would like to thank Vee Bostel and Sedgemoor Manor Community Junior School for their valuable contribution in the planning of this book.

# WAYS TO IMPROVE YOUR SPELLING

This book offers a number of ways to help you improve your spelling. There are listed here, along with a few other ideas you might like to try.

**1.** Learn the basic rules of spelling; there are some on page 304 of this book.

**2.** Use mnemonics, which are jingles or patterns which jog your memory, to help you remember words which you find difficult to spell. You will find them in many entries in this book. If you don't know or can't find one which exists for a particular word you want to remember, try making up your own. Examples of mnemonics are:

there's **a rat** in sep**arat**e

it is ne**cess**ary to have one **c**ollar (**c**) and two **s**ocks (**s**)

**3.** Break the word down into smaller parts, and learn each small part separately. This is recommended for a number of words in this book.

**4.** Visualize a difficult word. Try to remember its letters and the shape they make. This will give you a feel for whether a word looks right or wrong when you write it down.

**5.** Exaggerate the pronunciation of the word in your head. Sound out all the letters, including any silent letters.

**6.** Look at the word, cover it up, attempt to write it down, then check to see if you are correct. Keep doing this until you spell the word correctly.

**7.** Write out the word many times in your own handwriting, until you feel it flows without you hesitating.

**8.** If you spell a word wrongly, make a note of the error. You can learn to recognize the mistakes you tend to make and so prevent yourself from repeating them.

**9.** Make a habit of looking up any word which you are not absolutely sure about in a good dictionary.

# HOW TO USE THIS BOOK

**Headwords,** which are the words each entry is about, are shown in bold. Some have <u>underlined</u> parts to bring to your attention the part or parts of the word which people most often get wrong. These difficult areas are then spelt out further in the sentences which follow.

**Confusible words,** which are words that are alike in sound or spelling and can be mixed up easily, appear together as headwords. Short explanations and example phrases tell you which word or spelling you should use.

RULE These are spelling rules which help explain certain patterns in spelling. There is a list of these on page 304 of this book.

☆ This is a tip to help you remember how a word is spelt. This might be to break a word down into small parts or remember another related word which is easier to spell. A simple phrase might be used to show up a word inside a longer one, or the initial letters of each word of a sentence might spell the word out for you.

*US spellings* which are different from British spellings are included at the end of an entry. There is a section on American Spellings on page 311 of this book.

## abattoir

There is one **b** and two **t**s in abattoir.
The ending is **-oir**.

☆ Remember: There may be a **batt**le in an a**batt**oir.

## abbreviate

There are two **b**s in abbreviate.

Related words are
*adjective* **abbreviated**
*noun* **abbreviation**

RULE A final silent **E** is dropped when an ending which begins with a vowel is added:
***abbreviate+ion* > *abbreviat+ion* = *abbreviation***

## abhor

There is an **h** after the **b** in abhor.

Related words are
*adjective* **abhorrent**
*noun* **abhorrence**

RULE When an ending which begins with a vowel is added to a word which ends in a single vowel plus a consonant, the consonant is doubled if the *stress* is on the end of the word:

**abhor+ent** > **abhorr+ent** = **abhorrent**
**abhor+ence** > **abhorr+ence** = **abhorrence**

☆ Remember: You ab**hor** something **hor**rible.

## abscess
The first "ss" sound in abscess is spelt **sc**.
The last "ss" sound is spelt **ss**.

## absence
Absence is spelt with a single **s** at the beginning and a single **c** at the end.
The opposite of absence is also spelt this way:
**presence**

A related word is
*adjective* **absent**

A number of *adjectives* which end in **-ent** are related to *nouns* which end in **-ence**:
**absent** > **absence**

## abysmal
The vowel sound between **b** and **s** is spelt with a **y**.

A related word is
*adverb* **abysmally**

☆ Remember: Wh**y** can't you spell ab**y**smal?

## acc<u>e</u>lerate

There are two **c**s and one **l** in accelerate.
The vowel between **l** and **r** is **e**.

Related words are
 *noun* **acceleration**
 *noun* **accelerator**

RULE A final silent **E** is dropped when an ending which begins with a vowel is added:
 ***accelerate+ion > accelerat+ion = acceleration***
 ***accelerate+or > accelerat+or = accelerator***

☆ Remember: **A C**ar **C**an **E**asily **L**ead **E**very **R**ace.

## accept, except

These two words are often confused.

To **accept** something is to receive it or agree to it: *Please accept my apologies; The king would not accept their demands.*
To **accept** something is also to tolerate it: *He dutifully accepted his lot in life.*
To **accept** something is also to believe it is true: *I accept that a genuine error was made.*
**Except** means other than or apart from: *I never wear a skirt except when we go out.*

## accessory

There is a double **c** and a double **s** in accessory. The ending is **-ory**.

The *plural* of accessory is:
### accessories

RULE The *plural* of a word which ends in **y** is made by changing the **y** to **i** and adding **-es**:
### accessory > accessori+es = accessories

## accident

There are two **c**s in **accident**.

Related words are
*adjective* **accidental**
*adverb* **accidentally**

☆ Remember: **A c**lose **c**all can lead to an **acc**ident.

## accommodate

There are two **c**s and two **m**s in accommodate.

A related word is
*noun* **accommodation**

RULE A final silent **E** is dropped when an ending which begins with a vowel is added:
### accommodate+ion > accommodat+ion = accommodation

☆ Remember: The committee expands to

accommodate as many members as possible. (If you think of as many members as possible being **accommodated**, it may help you to remember that there are two **c**s <u>and</u> two **m**s).

## acc̲o̲m̲pany

There are two **c**s and one **m** in accompany.

Accompany is made up of the *noun* **company** plus the *prefix* **ac-** added at the beginning:

   *ac+company = accompany*

A related word is

   *noun* **accompaniment**

Accompaniment is made up of the *verb* **accompany** plus the *noun suffix* **-ment** added at the end.

RULE When an ending to a word which ends in a consonant plus **y**, the **y** changes to **i** (unless the ending added already begins with **i**):

   *accompany+ment > accompani+ment = accompaniment*

## acc̲u̲mulate

There are two **c**s and one **m** in accumulate.

A related word is

   *noun* **accumulation**

## accurate

There are two **c**s in accurate.
The ending is **-ate**.

A related word is
  noun **accuracy**

## ache

Ache is often combined with other words to make
new words:

  **back+ache = backache**
  **head+ache = headache**

☆ Remember: An **ache** needs **a che**ap remedy.
☆ Or: **A C**ut **H**urts **E**xtremely.
☆ Or break this word down into smaller parts to
help you remember the spelling:

  **a + ch + e**

## achieve

The **i** comes before the **e** in achieve.

RULE **I** before **E** except after **C**, when they make
the sound "ee".

A related word is
  noun **achievement**

## acknowledge

Acknowledge is made up of the noun **knowledge**
plus the prefix **ac-** added at the beginning:

*ac+knowledge = acknowledge*

A related word is
*noun* **acknowledgement** or **acknowledgment**

## acquaint
Acquaint begins with **acqu-**.

A related word is
*noun* **acquaintance**

The word is made up of the *verb* **acquaint** plus the *suffix* **-ance** added at the end:
*acquaint+ance = acquaintance*

## acquiesce
Acquiesce begins with **acqu-**.
The "ss" sound is spelt **sc**. The ending is **-sce**.

Related words are
*adjective* **acquiescent**
*noun* **acquiescence**

☆ Remember: Acquie**scent** ends in **scent**.

A number of *adjectives* which end in **-ent** are related to *nouns* which end in **-ence**:
*acquiescent > acquiescence*

## acquire
Acquire begins with **acqu-**.

## a**c**ross

There is a single **c** and a double **s** in across.

☆ Remember: You **cross** the road to go a**cross** it.

## a**dd**re**ss**

There is a double **d** and a double **s** in address.

☆ Remember: **Add** your **add**ress.

## adequate

The vowel after **d** in adequate is **e**.
The ending is **-ate**.

☆ Remember: **Equate** ad**equate** amounts.

## admit

The different *verb* forms of admit are:
   **admits**
   **admitted**
   **admitting**

Another related word is
   *noun* **admittance**

RULE When an ending which begins with a vowel
is added to a word which ends in a single vowel
plus a consonant, the consonant is doubled if the
*stress* is on the end of the word:
   **admit+ed > admitt+ed = admitted**
   **admit+ing > admitt+ing = admitting**

> ***admit+ance > admitt+ance = admittance***

## adolescent

The "ss" sound in adolescent is spelt **sc**.

Related words are
  noun ***adolescence***

A number of *adjectives* which end in **-ent** are related to *nouns* which end in **-ence**:
  ***adolescent > adolescence***

☆ Remember: Adole**scent** ends in **scent**.

## advantageous

There is an **e** after the **g** in advantageous.

RULE A final silent **E** is usually dropped when an ending which begins with a vowel is added. But this **E** is retained for the endings **-CE** or **-GE** when these letters keep a *soft* sound:
  ***advantage+ous = advantageous***

RULE The "uss" sound at the end of an *adjective* is almost always spelt **-OUS**.

## advertisement

There is an **e** after the **s** in advertisement.

RULE A final silent **E** is dropped when an ending which begins with a vowel is added, but may not be dropped when an ending which begins with a consonant is added:

### advertise+ment = advertisement

Even though the pronunciation of **advertise** changes when the *noun suffix* **-ment** is added, the spelling doesn't change.

## advice, advise

These two spellings are often confused.

**Advice**, with a **c**, is the *noun*: *Thanks for the advice.*

**Advise**, with an **s**, is the *verb*: *Please advise me what to do.*

Other words where **-ice** is the *noun*, and **-ise** is the *verb* are:

   noun **dev<u>ice</u>**
   verb **dev<u>ise</u>**
   noun **pract<u>ice</u>**
   verb **pract<u>ise</u>**

☆ Adv**ice** contains the *noun* **ice**, while adv**ise** contains the *verb* **is**.

## <u>ae</u>rial

Aerial begins with **ae-**.
The ending is **-al**.

## <u>ae</u>sthetic

Aesthetic begins with **ae-**.

*U.S. spelling (sometimes)*

*esthetic*

## affect, effect
These two words are often confused.

To **affect** something is to influence or change it: *Tiredness affected his concentration.*
An **effect** is a result something gives or an impression something makes: *discoveries which have a profound effect on medicine.*

☆ Remember: To **a**ffect something is to **a**lter it but an **e**ffect is the **e**nd result.

## affiliate
There are two **f**s and one **l** in affiliate.

A related word is
   noun **affiliation**

## aggravate
There are two **g**s in aggravate.
The vowel after **r** is **a**.

A related word is
   noun **aggravation**

RULE A final silent **E** is dropped when an ending which begins with a vowel is added:
   **aggravate+ion > aggravat+ion = aggravation**

## aggressive
There is a double **g** and a double **s** in aggressive.

A related word is
  *noun* **aggression**

## aghast
There is an **h** after **g** in aghast.

☆ Remember: a**gh**ast at the **gh**osts and **gh**ouls.

## agoraphobia
There is an **o** between the **g** and **r** in agoraphobia.

A related word is
  *adjective, noun* **agoraphobic**

☆ Remember: I was **ago**raphobic years **ago**.

## align
The ending of align is **-ign**, even though it is connected to the word line.

A related word is
  *noun* **alignment**

## allergy
There are two **l**s in allergy. The beginning is **all-**.
**All-** is followed by **er**.
The ending is **-gy**.

A related word is

*adjective* **allergic**

☆ Remember: An **allergy** saps **all** en**ergy**.

## alligator
There are two **l**s in alligator.
The vowel after **all-** is **i**.
The ending is **-or**.

## allow<u>ance</u>
There are two **l**s in allowance.
The ending is **-ance**, with an **a**.
The word is made up of the *verb* **allow** plus the *suffix* **-ance** added at the end:
 *allow+ance = allowance*

## all right
Although this is increasingly being spelt as one word, **alright**, it is still safest to spell it as two separate words, **all right**, as many people believe this is the only correct way to spell it.

## allude, elude
These two words are often confused.

To **allude** to something is to refer to it in an indirect way: *I never allude to an unpleasant matter.*
If something **eludes** you, you can't understand or remember it: *The name of the tune eludes me.*

If you **elude** something, you dodge or escape from it: *She managed to elude the police.*

☆ Remember: If something **e**ludes you it **e**scapes you.

## almond

There is a silent **l** after the **a** in almond.

## already

There is only one **l** in already.

RULE When **AL-** is added as a *prefix* at the beginning of a word to make a new word, it is spelt with one **L**:

*al+ready = already*

**Already** is spelt as one word, not two, when it means happening before the present or before expected: *My uncle was already away.*
You need to use two words when each word carries meaning: *She's all ready to go.*

## altar, alter

These two words are sometimes confused.

An **altar** is a holy table in a church or temple.
To **alter** something is to change it.

☆ Remember: **Alter** to the **alter**native.

## although

There is only one **l** in although.

RULE When **AL-** is added as a *prefix* at the beginning of a word to make a new word, it is spelt with one **L**:

*al+though = although*

## altogether

There is only one **l** in altogether.

RULE When **AL-** is added as a *prefix* at the beginning of a word to make a new word, it is spelt with one **L**:

*al+together = altogether*

**Altogether** is spelt as one word, not two, when it means completely or in total: *She wasn't altogether pleased to see them.*
You need to use two words when each word carries meaning: *I just can't wait until we're all together.*

## aluminium

The vowel after **l** in aluminium is **u**.
The ending is **-ium**.

☆ Break this word down into smaller parts to help you remember the spelling:

*a + lu + mi + ni + um*

*U.S. and Canadian spelling*
  ***aluminum***

## amateur
The ending of amateur is **-eur**.

## amethyst
The vowel after **m** in amethyst is **e**.
The ending is **-yst**.

## anaesthetic
The vowel sound between **n** and **s** in anaesthetic
is spelt **ae**.

## analyse
The final vowel sound in analyse is spelt **y**.
The ending is **-yse**.

Related words are
  *noun **analysis***
  *noun **analyst***

*U.S. spelling*
  ***analyze***

## ancestor
The "ss" sound after **an-** in ancestor is spelt **c**.
The ending is **-or**.

A related word is
  *noun **ancestry***

## annihilate
There is a double **n** in annihilate.
The vowel following the double **n** is **i**.
There is an **h** after **anni-**.

A related word is
   *noun* **annihilation**

☆ Break this word down into smaller parts to help
you remember the spelling:
   *an + ni + hi + late*

## announcement
There is an **e** after the **c** in announcement.

Rᴜʟᴇ A final silent **ᴇ** is dropped when an ending
which begins with a vowel is added, but may not
be dropped when an ending which begins with a
consonant is added:
   *announce+ment = announcement*

## anonymous
The vowel after **n** in anonymous is **y**.
The ending is **-ous**.

Rᴜʟᴇ The "uss" sound at the end of an *adjective* is
almost always spelt **-ous**.

A related word is
   *noun* **anonymity**

☆ Remember: You use a pseudo**nym** to stay
ano**nym**ous.

## answer
There is a silent **w** after **s** in answer.

A related word is
*verb, adjective **answered***

☆ Break these words down into parts to help you remember the spellings:
*an + swer*
*an + swer + ed*

## Antarctic
There is a **c** between the **r** and **t** of Antarctic.
It also appears in the word:
**Arctic**

☆ Remember: There is an **arc** in the Ant**arc**tic.

## anxious
There is no **g** in anxious.
The "sh" sound is spelt **xi**.

RULE The "uss" sound at the end of an *adjective* is almost always spelt **-ous**.

A related word is
*noun **anxiety***

## apologize *or* apologise
The middle letter of apologize is **o**.

☆ Remember: I will **log** an apo**log**y.

## appal

There are two **p**s in appal.
There is only one **l** at the end.

A related word is
*adjective* **appalling**

RULE When an ending which begins with a vowel
is added to a word which ends in a single vowel
plus **l**, the **l** is doubled:

*appal+ing > appall+ing = appalling*

## apparatus

There are two **p**s in apparatus.
The vowel after **pp** is **a**.
The ending is **-us**.

## apparent

There are two **p**s in apparent.
The ending is **-ent**.

A related word is
*adverb* **apparently**

☆ Remember: Something which **app**ears is
**app**arent.

## appearance

There are two **p**s in appearance.
The ending is **-ance**.

## appendix
There are two **p**s in appendix.

A related word is
  noun **appendicitis**

The vowel after **d** in appendicitis is **i**.
The **x** of appendix changes to **c** to give the "ss" sound.

☆ If you remember that appendicitis is a disease of the **appendix**, it may help you to remember that the vowel after **d** is **i**.

## appl**iance**
There are two **p**s in appliance.
The ending is **-ance**.

RULE When an ending is added to a word that ends in a consonant plus **y**, the **y** changes to **i** (unless the ending added already begins with **i**):
  *apply+ance > appli+ance = appliance*

## appre**ci**ate
There are two **p**s in appreciate.
The "shi" or "si" sound (depending upon how you pronounce the word) is spelt **ci**.

Related words are
  noun **appreciation**
  adjective **appreciative**

RULE A final silent **E** is dropped when an ending

which begins with a vowel is added:

**appreciate+ion > appreciat+ion =
appreciation
appreciate+ive > appreciat+ive =
appreciative**

☆ Remember: you should ap**preci**ate **preci**ous things.

☆ Or break the word down into smaller parts to help you remember the spelling:

*ap + pre + ci + ate*

## apprehensive

There is a double **p** at the beginning of apprehensive. The beginning is **app-**.
The vowel after **r** is **e**.

Related words are
*noun* **apprehension**
*verb* **apprehend**

☆ Break the word down into smaller parts to help you remember the spelling:

*ap + pre + hen + sive*

## approve

There are two **p**s in approve.

A related word is
*noun* **approval**

## approximate

There are two **p**s in approximate.

A related word is
*adverb* **approximately**

## arbitrary

There is an **r** after the **t** in arbitrary which is sometimes missed out in speech.

Related words are
*noun* **arbitration**
*verb* **arbitrate**

☆ Remember: It is cont**rary** to be arbit**rary**.

## archaeology

The "k" sound in archaeology is spelt **ch**.
The vowel sound between **ch** and **o** is spelt **ae**.

A related word is
*noun* **archaeologist**

☆ Remember: Ar**chae**ology discovers **c**urious **h**ouses of **a**ncient **e**ras.

## architect

The "k" sound in architect is spelt **ch**.

A related word is
*noun* **architecture**

Architecture ends in the *noun suffix* **-ure**.

## Ar<u>c</u>tic

There is a **c** between the **r** and **t** of Arctic.
It also appears in the word:

   ***Antar<u>c</u>tic***

☆ Remember: There is an **arc** in the **Arc**tic.

## argue

The different *verb* forms of argue are:

   ***argues***
   ***arguing***
   ***argued***

Other related words are
   *adjective* ***arguable***
   *adverb* ***arguably***

RULE  A final silent **E** is dropped when an ending which begins with a vowel is added:

   ***argue+ed > argu+ed = argued***
   ***argue+ing > argu+ing = arguing***
   ***argue+able > argu+able = arguable***
   ***argue+ably > argu+ably = arguably***

Another related word is
   *noun* ***argument***

Usually, a final silent **e** is dropped when an ending which begins with a vowel is added, but may not be dropped when an ending which begins with a consonant is added. However, in argument the **e** <u>is</u> dropped:

*argue+ment > argu+ment = argument*

## arrangement
There is an **e** after the **g** in arrangement.

RULE A final silent **E** is dropped when an ending which begins with a vowel is added, but may not be dropped when an ending which begins with a consonant is added:

*arrange+ment = arrangement*

## article
The vowel after **t** in article is **i**.
The ending is **-cle**.

## artificial
The "sh" sound in artificial is spelt **ci**.
The ending is **-cial**.

## ascend
The "ss" sound in ascend is spelt **sc**.
The opposite of ascend is also spelt with **sc**:
*descend*

A related word is
*noun* **ascent**

☆ Remember: A**sc**end by the e**sc**alator.

## assassinate
There are two sets of double **s** in assassinate.

Related words are
  noun **assassin**
  noun **assassination**

RULE  A final silent **E** is dropped when an ending
which begins with a vowel is added:
  **assassinate+ion > assassinat+ion =
  assassination**

## assess
There are two sets of double **s** in assess.

A related word is
  noun **assessment**

☆ Remember: Only an **ass** will gu**ess** and not
**ass**ess.

## assist
There is a double **s** in assist.

A related word is
  noun **assistance**
  noun **assistant**

## associate
The first "ss" sound in associate is spelt **ss**.
The second "ss" sound is spelt with a single **c**.

A related word is
  noun **association**

## asthma
Asthma begins with **as-**.
There is a **th** in the middle.

A related word is
*adjective, noun* **asthmatic**

☆ Break this word down into smaller parts to help
you remember the spelling:

*as + th + ma*

## atheist
The **e** comes before the **i** in atheist.

A related word is
*noun* **atheism**

## athlete •
There is no vowel between **h** and **l** in athlete.

A related word is
*adjective* **athletic**

## atrocious
The "sh" sound in atrocious is spelt **ci**.
The ending is **-ous**.

RULE The "uss" sound at the end of an *adjective* is
almost always spelt **-ous**.

A related word is
*noun* **atrocity**

## attach

At<u>t</u>ach has a double **t** at the beginning.
There is no **t** at the end, just **-ch**.
The opposite of attach is also spelt with **-ch**:
   *deta<u>ch</u>*

☆ Remember: Att**ach** **a** **c**oat **h**ook to the wall.

## attendant

Attendant has a double **t** at the beginning.
The ending is **-ant**.

A related word is
   *noun* **attendance**

☆ Remember: You **dance** atten**dance** on someone.

## attitude

There is a double **t** at the beginning of attitude.
The vowel following **tt** is **i**.
There is a single **t** at the end. The ending is **-tude**.

☆ Remember: You have a bad **atti**tude **at ti**mes.

## autograph

The vowel after **t** in aut<u>o</u>graph is **o**.

## automatic

The vowel after **t** in aut<u>o</u>matic is **o**.

☆ Remember: an **auto**matic **auto**mobile

## autum<u>n</u>
There is a silent **n** at the end of autumn.

☆ Remember: I am solem**n**ly condem**n**ed to build a colum**n** in the autum**n**.

## auxil<u>i</u>ary
There is an **i** after the **l** in auxiliary. The ending is **-iary**.

## awful
There is no **e** in awful, even though it is related to the word awe.
The ending is **-ful**.

RULE  The *suffix* **-FUL** is always spelt with one **L**.

# B

## bachelor
There is no **t** in bachelor, just **ch**.
The ending is **-or**.

☆ Remember: Was **Bach** a **bach**elor?

## baggage
There is a double **g** in baggage.
A similar word with double **g** is:
*luggage*

**RULE** When an ending which begins with a vowel is added to a word which ends in a single vowel plus a consonant, the consonant is doubled if the *stress* is on the end of the word or if the word has only one part:

*bag+age > bagg+age = baggage*

## balloon
There are two **l**s in balloon.

☆ Remember that balloon contains the word **ball**.

## banana
Banana has two single **n**s.

☆ Break the word down into small parts ending in **a** to help you remember the spelling:

*ba + na + na*

## bankruptcy
There is a **t** before the **-cy** in bankruptcy which is sometimes missed out in speech.

Bankruptcy is made up of the *adjective* **bankrupt** plus the *noun suffix* **-cy** added at the end:

*bankrupt+cy = bankruptcy*

## barbecue
The vowel after **barb-** is **e**.
The ending is **-cue**.

☆ Remember that barbecue can be broken down into three small words:

*bar + be + cue*

## basically
Basically ends in **-ally**.

☆ Remember: **Ally** and S**ally** are basic**ally** p**ally**.

## bated, baited
These two words sound the same and they are often confused.

You wait with **bated** breath.
**Baited** is the *past tense* of **bait**: *The trap had been baited.*

## battalion

There are two **t**s and one **l** in battalion.

☆ Remember: There are two **t**s and one **l** in **battalion**, and two **t**s and one **l** in **battle**.

## beauty

Beauty contains a sequence of three vowels, **eau**.

☆ Remember: **B**ig **E**ars **A**re **U**seful **T**o **Y**ou.

A related word is
    *adjective* **beautiful**

RULE When an ending is added to a word that ends in a consonant plus **y**, the **y** changes to **i** (unless the ending added already begins with **i**):
    *beauty+ful > beauti+ful = beautiful*

RULE The *suffix* -FUL is always spelt with one **L**.

☆ Remember: **B**ig **E**lephants **A**re **U**sually **beau**tiful.

☆ Or: **B**ig **E**lephants **A**re **U**seful **T**o **I**ndians **F**or **U**nloading **L**ogs.

## beggar

The ending of beggar is **-ar**.

☆ Remember: There is a beg**gar** in the **gar**den.

## beginner

There is a double **n** in beginner.

A related word is
*noun, verb* **beginning**

RULE When an ending which begins with a vowel is added to a word which ends in a single vowel plus a consonant, the consonant is doubled if the *stress* is on the end of the word:

*begin+er > beginn+er = beginner*
*begin+ing > beginn+ing = beginning*

## behaviour

There is no **e** after the **v** in behaviour.
There is an **i** before the **-our** ending.

RULE A final silent **E** is dropped when an ending which begins with a vowel is added:

*behave+iour > behav+iour = behaviour*

## believe

The first vowel sound in believe is spelt with a single **e**.
The **i** comes before the **e** in the vowel sound after **l**.

Rule I before **E** except after **C**, when they make the sound "ee".

A related word is
  *adjective* **believable**

Rule A final silent **E** is dropped when an ending which begins with a vowel is added:
  *believe+able > believ+able = believable*

# belligerent
There are two **l**s in belligerent.

# beneficial
The "sh" sound in beneficial is spelt **ci**. The ending is **-cial**.

# benefit
The different *verb* forms of benefit are:
  **benefits**
  **benefited**
  **benefiting**

Rule When an ending which begins with a vowel is added to a word which ends in a single vowel plus a consonant, the consonant is doubled if the *stress* is on the end of the word.

The stress in benefit is not on the end of the word, therefore:
  *benefit+ed = benefited*
  *benefit+ing = benefiting*

# berserk

There is an **r** after **be-** in berserk which is sometimes missed out in speech.

☆ Break the word down into smaller parts to help you remember the spelling:
*ber + ser + k*

# bias

Bias ends in a single **s**.

The different *verb* forms of bias are:
**biases** *or* **biasses**
**biasing** *or* **biassing**
**biased** *or* **biassed**

Another related word is
*adjective* **biased** *or* **biassed**

All the above forms are correct, but the forms with a single **s** are more common.

The *plural* of bias is
**biases**

RULE The *plural* of a word which ends in **s**, **x**, **z**, **sh**, or **ch** is made by adding -**es**:
*bias+es = biases*

# biscuit

The ending of biscuit is -**cuit**.

☆ Break the word down into smaller parts to help

you remember the spelling:
> *bis + cu + it*

☆ Remember: If you want a bisc**uit** I will give **u** (you) **it**.

## blasphemy
The "f" sound in blasphemy is spelt **ph**.

A related word is
> *adjective* **blasphemous**

## born, borne
These two spellings are often confused.

To be **born** is to be brought into life.
To be **borne** is to be accepted or carried: *He has borne his illness with courage.*
When fruit or flowers are **borne** by a plant, they are produced by it: *The trees have borne fruit.*
If something is **borne** out, it is confirmed: *The predictions have been borne out by the election results.*

## bou̲lder
The "oh" sound in boulder is spelt **ou**.

☆ Remember: The b**oulder** hit my sh**oulder**.

## bound̲a̲ry
The ending of boundary is **-ary**.

## bouquet

The "oo" sound in bouquet is spelt **ou**.
The "k" sound is spelt **qu**.
The ending is **-et**.

☆ Remember: The **Que**en was given a bou**que**t.

## bourgeois

The "oo" sound in bourgeois is spelt **ou**.
The "dj" sound is spelt **g**.
The ending is **-eios**.

A related word is
   noun **bourgeoisie**

## bow, bough

These words sound the same and they can be confused.

To **bow** is to bend your body or head.
A **bow** is an action where you bend your body or head.
A **bough** is a branch of a tree.

## boycott

There are two **t**s at the end of boycott.

## braille

The "ay" sound in braille is spelt **ai**.
There are two **l**s.
There is an **e** at the end.

## breach, breech
These words sound the same and they can be confused.

To **breach** something is to break or break through it: *breach of the peace.*
A **breach** is a break or a gap made.
The **breech** is the lower part of a human body or some other thing: *a breech birth.*

## breadth
The vowel sound in breadth is spelt **ea**, even though it is related to the word **broad**.
The ending of breadth is **-dth**.

## breath, breathe
These two spellings are often confused.

**Breath**, without an **e**, is the *noun*: *He took a deep breath.*
**Breathe**, with an **e**, is the *verb*: *I heard him breathe a sigh of relief.*

## breathalyse
The vowel after **breath** in breathalyse is **a**.
The ending is **-yse**.

☆ Remember: The police breath**alyse** you to an**alyse** the sample.

*U.S. spelling*
  **breathalyze**

## brief

The **i** comes before the **e** in brief.

RULE **I** before **E** except after **C**, when they make the sound "ee".

## brigadier

The **i** comes before the **e** in brigadier. The ending is **-ier**.

RULE **I** before **E** except after **C**, when they make the sound "ee".

## Britain

**Britain** is spelt with a capital **B**.

RULE The name or names of a country or other area on the map begin with a capital letter.

The second vowel sound is spelt **ai**. The ending is **-ain**.

☆ Remember: There is a lot of r**ain** in Brit**ain**.

## broad

The vowel sound in broad is spelt **oa**.

A related word is
  noun **breadth**

☆ Remember: a b**road road**

## broccoli
There are two **c**s and one **l** in broccoli.

☆ Remember: Bro**cc**oli **c**ures **coli**c.

## brochure
The "sh" sound in brochure is spelt **ch**.
The ending is **-ure**.

## bronchial
The "k" sound in bronchial is spelt **ch**.

A related word is
  *noun* **bronchitis**

## bruise
The "oo" sound in bruise is spelt **ui**.
The ending is **-se**.

## brusque
The "oo" sound in brusque is spelt **u**.
The ending is **-que**.

## Buddhism
Buddhism is spelt with a capital **B**.

Related words are
  *noun* **Buddhist**
  *noun* **Buddha**

RULE The name of a religious group or its teachings begins with a capital letter.

## bulletin

There are two **l**s and one **t** in bulletin.

## buoy

Buoy, meaning a floating object attached to the bottom of the sea, is spelt with a **u** after the **b**.

This spelling can be confused with **boy**.

☆ Remember: a **B**ig **U**nsinkable **O**bject **Y**oked in the sea

## buoyant

Buoyant is spelt with a **u** after the **b**.
The ending is **-ant**.

A related word is
*noun* **buoyancy**

☆ Remember: **B**ig **U**nsinkable **O**bjects **Y**oked **AN**d **T**ied

## bureau

Bureau begins with **bu-**.
The ending is **-eau**.

RULE The *plural* of a word which ends in **-EAU** is made by adding **s** or **x**:
**bureaus** *or* **bureaux**

☆ Remember: **B**usinesses **U**sing **R**otten **E**thics **A**re **U**seless.

## bureaucracy

Bureaucracy begins with **bur-**.
The vowel sound after **r** is spelt **eau**.
The ending is **-acy**.

A related word is
  noun **bureaucrat**
  adjective **bureaucratic**

☆ Remember: **B**usinesses **U**sing **R**otten **E**thics **A**re **U**seless.
☆ Or break this word down into smaller parts to help you remember the spelling:
  *bu + reau + cra + cy*

## burglar

Burglar ends in **-ar**.

A related word is
  noun **burglary**

☆ Remember: There is a burgl**ar** in the g**ar**den.

## bus

The *plural* of bus is:
  *buses* or (rarely) *busses*

RULE The *plural* of a word which ends in **s**, **x**, **z**, **sh**, or **ch** is made by adding **-es**.

The different *verb* forms of bus are:
  *buses* or more rarely *busses*
  *busing* or more rarely *bussing*

*bused* or more rarely *bussed*

## bus<u>i</u>ness
There is an **i** in the middle of business.
The first vowel is **u**.

☆ Remember: It's none of your **bus**iness what
**bus I** get!

# C

## caffeine
There are two **f**s in caffeine.
The **e** comes before the **i**.

RULE Usually **I** comes before **E** except after **C**, when they make the sound "ee".

However, **caffeine** is an <u>exception</u> to this rule, with the **e** before the **i**.

## calendar
In calendar the first vowel is **a**, the second is **e**, and the last is **a**:
The ending is **-ar**.

This spelling can be confused with **colander**, meaning a drainer.

☆ Remember: The cal**endar** marks the **end** of the ye**ar**.
☆ Or break this word down into smaller parts to help you remember the spelling:
   *cal + en + dar*

## cam<u>ou</u>fl<u>age</u>
The vowel sound after **m** in camouflage is spelt **ou**.
The ending is **-age**.

## campaign
Campaign ends in **-gn**.

## cancel
The *verb* forms of cancel are:
**cancels**
**cancelled**
**cancelling**

A related word is
*noun* **cancellation**

RULE When an ending which begins with a vowel is added to a word which ends in a single vowel plus **L**, the **L** is doubled:
**cancel+ed > cancell+ed = cancelled**
**cancel+ing > cancell+ing = cancelling**
**cancel+ation > cancell+ation = cancellation**

## canvas, canvass
These words sound the same and they are often confused.

**Canvas** is strong cloth.
To **canvass** is to persuade people to vote a

particular way or to find out their opinions about
something.

☆ Remember that if you canva**ss** you **s**eek
**s**omething.

## carbohydrate
The vowel after **carb-** in carbohydrate is **o**. The
beginning is **carbo-**.

☆ Remember that **carbo**hydrates contain
**carbo**n.

## career
There is one **r** in the middle of career.

The different *verb* forms of career are:
> *careers*
> *careering*
> *careered*

☆ Remember: A **car car**eered off the road.

## careful
There is an **e** after the **r** in careful.
There is one **l** at the end.

The word is made up of the *noun* **care** plus the
*suffix* **-ful** added at the end:
> *care+ful = careful*

RULE The *suffix* **-FUL** is always spelt with one **L**.

## carnivorous

The vowel after **v** in carnivorous is **o**.

A related word is
noun **carnivore**

☆ If you remember that carnivorous is related to the word carniv**o**re, where the **o** is more pronounced, it may help you to remember that the vowel after **v** in carniv**o**rous is **o**.

## carriage

There is an **i** in carriage before **-age**.
This word has the same ending as:
**marriage**

RULE When an ending is added to a word which ends in a consonant plus **y**, the **y** changes to **i** (unless the ending added already begins with **i**):
**carry+age > carri+age = carriage**

## cashier

The **e** comes before the **i** in cashier.

RULE **i** before **E** except after **c**, when they make the sound "ee".

## cassette

There is a double **s** and a double **t** in cassette.

## casualty

There is an **a** after the **u** in casualty.

☆ Break this word down into smaller parts to help
you remember the spelling:
   *ca + su + al + ty*

## catalogue

The last two letters of catalogue are **-ue**. The
ending is **-gue**.

*U.S. spelling (sometimes)*
   **catalog**

## catarrh

There is one **t** in catarrh.
The ending is **-rrh**.

☆ Remember the similarity between the words
cata**rrh**, dia**rrh**oea, and haemo**rrh**age.

## category

The vowel after the **t** in category is **e**.

## cauliflower

The "aw" sound in cauliflower is spelt **au**. The first
part is **cauli-**.
The last part is **-flower**.

## cautious

The "aw" sound in cautious is spelt **au**.

The "sh" sound is spelt **ti**.
The ending is **-ous**.

RULE The "uss" sound at the end of an *adjective* is almost always spelt **-ous**.

A related word is
  noun ***caution***

## ceiling
Ceiling begins with a **c**.
The **e** comes before the **i**.

RULE **I** before **E** except after **c**, when they make the sound "ee".

## celebrate
The vowel after **l** in celebrate is **e**.

A related word is
  noun ***celebration***

☆ Remember: The **cele**brity **cele**brated.
☆ Or break this word down into smaller parts to help you remember the spelling:
  ***ce + le + brate***

## cellophane
Cellophane begins with **c**.
There is a double **l**.
The vowel after **ll** is **o**.
The "f" sound is spelt **ph**.

☆ Break this word down into smaller parts to help you remember the spelling:

   *cell + o + phane*

## cemet<u>ery</u>

Cemetery begins with **c**.
Every vowel is **e**.
The ending is **-ery**.

☆ Remember: a v**ery** grim cemet**ery**
☆ Or remember that there are three **e**s in c**e**m**e**t**e**ry.
☆ Or break this word down into smaller parts to help you remember the spelling:

   *ce + me + te + ry*

## cen<u>tre</u>

Centre ends in **-tre**.

*U.S. spelling*
   **center**

## cereal, serial

These two spellings are often confused.

**Cereal** is food made from grain.
A **serial** is something published or broadcast in a number of parts.
**Serial** also describes other things that happen in a **series**.

Cereal begins with **ce-**.

The ending is **-eal**.

☆ Remember: Ce**real** is a **real** breakfast.

## cert**ai**n
The vowel after **t** in certain is spelt **ai**.

Related words are
 adverb **certainly**
 noun **certainty**

☆ Remember: It is cert**ain** to r**ain** in Sp**ain**.

## champ**agne**
Champagne begins with **ch**.
The "ay" sound is spelt **a**.
The ending is **-gne**.

☆ Remember: **Agnes** thinks champ**agne** and las**agne** go together.

## chang**e**able
There is an **e** after **g** in changeable.

RULE A final silent **E** is usually dropped when an ending which begins with a vowel is added. But this **E** is retained for the endings **-CE** or **-GE** when these letters keep a *soft* sound:
 ***change+able = changeable***

## **ch**aos
The "k" sound at the beginning of chaos is spelt **ch**.

The "ay" sound is spelt **a**.
There is a single **s** at the end. The ending is **-os**.

A related word is
*adjective* **chaotic**

☆ Remember: **C**itizens **H**ave **A**bolished **O**ur **S**ystem.

## character

Character begins with **ch-**.
The vowel after **r** is **a**.
The ending is **-er**.

A related word is
*noun, adjective* **characteristic**

☆ Break this word down into smaller parts to help you remember the spelling:

*cha + rac + ter*

## chauffeur

This is a word which came into English from French.

The "sh" sound in chauffeur is spelt **ch**.
The "oh" sound is spelt **au**.
There is a double **f** in the middle.
The ending is **-eur**.

☆ Break this word down into smaller parts to help you remember the spelling:

*ch + au + ff + eur*

## cheetah
The "ee" sound in cheetah is spelt **ee**.
The ending is **-ah**.

This word should not be confused with the spelling of **cheat** or **cheater**.

## chord, cord
These two spellings are often confused.

A **chord** is a group of three or more musical notes played together.
**Cord** is strong thick string or electrical wire.
Your vocal **cords** are folds in your throat which are used to produce sound.

☆ Remember: A **chord** is played in **chor**us.

## chute
The "sh" sound in chute is spelt **ch**.
The "oo" sound is spelt **u**, with a final silent **e**.

This word, which is a steep slope for sliding things down, sounds the same as **shoot** and is often confused with it.

## cigarette
There is an **a** after the **g** in cigarette which is sometimes missed out in speech.

The word is made up of the *noun* **cigar** plus the *suffix* **-ette** added at the end:
  ***cigar+ette = cigarette***

# cinnamon
There is a double **n** and a single **m** in cinnamon.

# cistern
Cistern begins with **c**.
The ending is **-ern**.

# claustrophobia
The "aw" sound in claustrophobia is spelt **au**.
The vowel between **r** and **p** is **o**.

A related word is
  *adjective, noun* **claustrophobic**

☆ Remember: Claustrophobia is the fear of being closed in.

# cocoa
There is an **a** at the end of cocoa.
There is no **a** in the middle.

# coconut
There is no **a** in coconut.

# coffee
There is a double **f** in the middle of coffee.
There is a double **e** at the end.

☆ Remember: Co**ffee** and to**ffee** have a double **f** and a double **e**.

## coincidence

Coincidence is made up of the *noun* **incidence** plus the *prefix* **co-** added at the beginning:

**co+incidence = coincidence**

The "ss" sound in the middle is spelt **c**.
The ending is **-ence**.

A related word is
*adjective* **coincidental**

☆ Break these words down into smaller parts to help you remember their spellings:

**co + in + ci + dence**
**co + in + ci + dent + al**

## colander

There is one **l** in colander.
The ending is **-er**.

This word, meaning a bowl-shaped drainer, can be confused with **calendar**, a date chart.

☆ Remember: A col**and**er has h**and**les and drains wat**er**, the cal**end**ar marks the **end** of the ye**ar**.

## collaborate

There are two **l**s in collaborate.

The vowel after **b** is **o**.

Related words are
  noun **collaboration**
  noun **collaborator**

## collapsible
There are two **l**s in collapsible.
The ending is **-ible**.

## colleague
There are two **l**s in colleague.
The "ee" sound is spelt **ea**.
The ending is **-gue**.

☆ Remember: a **league** of col**league**s

## colonel
Colonel is spelt very differently from the way it sounds.

☆ Break this word down into smaller parts to help you remember the spelling:
  *co + lo + nel*

☆ Or remember: a **lone** co**lone**l

## colossal
There is a single **l** and a double **s** in colossal.
The ending is **-al**.

☆ Remember: co**loss**al **loss**es

## colour

The beginning of colour is **col-**.
The ending is **-our**.

A related word is
*adjective* **colourful**

RULE The *suffix* **-FUL** is always spelt with one **L**.

☆ Remember: **Our** fav**our**ite col**our**s are c**ol**d c**ol**ours.

*U.S. spellings*
**color**
**colorful**

## column

There is a silent **n** at the end of column.

☆ Remember: I am solem**n**ly condem**n**ed to build a colum**n** in the autum**n**.

## commemorate

There is a double **m** followed by a single **m** in commemorate.
There is an **o** between the **m** and the **r**.

A related word is
*noun* **commemoration**

## commercial

There are two **m**s in commercial.
The "sh" sound is spelt **ci**.

The ending is **-al**.

☆ Remember: A spe**cial** offi**cial** commer**cial** is cru**cial**.

## commi<u>se</u>rate

There are two **m**s and one **s** in commiserate.
The vowel after **s** is **e**.

A related word is
*noun* **commiseration**

☆ Remember: You **commiser**ate when someone **commi**ts a **ser**ious mistake.

## commit

There are two **m**s in commit.
The different *verb* forms of commit are:

*commits*
*committed*
*committing*

RULE When an ending which begins with a vowel is added to a word which ends in a single vowel plus a consonant, the consonant is doubled if the *stress* is on the end of the word:

*commit+ed > committ+ed = committed*
*commit+ing > committ+ing = committing*

A related word is
*noun* **commitment**

The final consonant may not be doubled when an ending which begins with a consonant is added:
*commit+ment = commitment*

## committee
There are two **m**s, two **t**s, and two **e**s in committee.

☆ Remember: The committee expands to accommodate to as many members as possible. (If you think of the **committee** as having as many members as possible, it may help you to remember that there are two **m**s, two **t**s, <u>and</u> two **e**s.)

## comparative
The letter between **r** and **t** in comparative is **a**. This is different from **comparison**, which has an **i**.

A related word is
*adverb* **comparatively**

☆ Remember: There is a **rat** in compa**rat**ive.

## comparison
The letter between **r** and **s** in comparison is **i**. This is different from **comparative**, which has an **a**.

☆ Remember that you make a com**parison** to

see if something **is on a par** with something else.
☆ Or: There's no com**paris**on with **Paris**.

## compat**ible**

The ending of compatible is **-ible**.

A related word is
   noun **compatibility**

RULE An *adjective* ending in **-IBLE** will form a *noun*
spelt **-IBILITY**, and an *adjective* ending in **-ABLE** will
form a *noun* spelt **-ABILITY**:
   *compatible > compatibility*

## compel

There is one **l** at the end of compel.
The different *verb* forms of compel are:
   *compels*
   *compelling*
   *compelled*

RULE When an ending which begins with a vowel
is added to a word which ends in a single vowel
plus **L**, the **L** is doubled:
   *compel+ing > compell+ing = compelling*
   *compel+ed > compell+ed = compelled*

## comp**e**tent

The middle vowel in competent is **e**.
The ending is **-ent**.

A related word is
  noun **competence**

☆ Remember: You must be **compete**nt in order to **compete**.

## competition

The vowel after **p** in competition is **e**.

Related words are
  adjective **competitive**
  noun **competitor**

☆ Remember that the word competition is related to the words **competitive** and **competitor**, where the **e** is more pronounced.

## complement, compliment

These words sound the same and they are often confused.

A **complement** is something which goes well with another or completes it: *She is a perfect complement to her husband.*
To **complement** something is to go well with it or complete it.
A **compliment** is a remark expressing admiration: *It's always good to pass the odd compliment.*
To **compliment** something is to express admiration for it.

☆ Remember: A compl**i**ment is the opposite of

an **i**nsult and a compl**e**ment compl**e**tes something.

## comple**x**ion
There is an **x** in complexion.

☆ Remember: X marks the spot!

## con**c**ede
The "ss" sound in concede is spelt with a single **c**. The ending is **-ede**.

## conc**ei**t
The **e** comes before the **i** in conceit.

RULE **I** before **E** except after **C**, when they make the sound "ee".

## conc**ei**ve
The **e** comes before the **i** in conceive.

RULE **I** before **E** except after **C**, when they make the sound "ee".

A related word is
*adjective* **conceivable**

RULE A final silent **E** is dropped when an ending which begins with a vowel is added:
*conceive+able > conceiv+able = conceivable*

## condem<u>n</u>

There is a silent **n** at the end of condemn.

A related word is
  noun **condemnation**

☆ If you remember that condemn is related to the word condem**n**ation, where the **n** is pronounced, it may help you to remember the **n** in condem**n**.

☆ Or remember: Condem**n** the **n** to the end.

☆ Or: I am solem**n**ly condem**n**ed to build a colum**n** in the autum**n**.

## conf<u>e</u>rence

There is an **e** after the **f** in conference which is sometimes missed out in speech.

The word is made up of the *verb* **confer** plus the *noun suffix* **-ence**:
  *confer+ence = conference*

☆ Remember: A **confer**ence is where you **confer**.

## con<u>geal</u>

The "j" sound in congeal is spelt **g**.

The ending is **-eal**.

☆ Remember: When your bone con**geal**s it **g**els and h**eal**s.

## connoisseur

This is a word which came into English from French.

There is a double **n** and a double **s** in connoisseur.
The middle vowel is spelt **oi**.
The ending is the French **-eur**.

## connotation

There is a double **n** in connotation.
The vowel after **nn** is **o**.

The word is made up of the *noun* **notation** plus the *prefix* **con-** added at the beginning. When the prefix **con-** is added to a word which begins with **n**, there will be two **n**s:

*con+notation = connotation*

## conscience

The "sh" sound in conscience is spelt **sci**.
A similar word with **sci** is:

*conscientious*

The final letters are exactly the same as the word **science**.

## conscientious

The first "sh" sound in conscientious is spelt **sci**.
A similar word with **sci** is:

*conscience*

The second "sh" sound is spelt **ti**.

RULE The "uss" sound at the end of an *adjective* is almost always spelt **-ous**.

## conscious
The "sh" sound in conscious is spelt **sci**.

RULE The "uss" sound at the end of an *adjective* is almost always spelt **-ous**.

## contemporary
There is an **o** in contemporary, between **p** and **r**, which is sometimes missed out in speech.
The ending is the same as in:
   *temporary*

## continent
Continent ends in **-ent**.

☆ Remember: I sp**ent** c**ent**s in another contin**ent**.

## control
There is one **l** at the end of control.

The different *verb* forms of control are:
   *controls*
   *controlling*
   *controlled*

RULE When an ending which begins with a vowel

is added to a word which ends in a single vowel plus **L**, the **L** is doubled:

> *control+ing > controll+ing = controlling*
> *control+ed > controll+ed = controlled*

## controversy

The vowel before **v** in controversy is **o**.

A related word is
> *adjective* **controversial**

RULE When an ending is added to a word which ends in a consonant plus **y**, the **y** changes to **i** (unless the ending added already begins with **i**):

> *controversy+al > controversi+al =*
> *controversial*

## convalesce

The "ss" sound in convalesce is spelt **sc**. The ending is **-sce**.

Related words are
> *adjective* **convalescent**
> *noun* **convalescence**

☆ Remember: Convale**scent** ends in **scent**.

A number of *adjectives* which end in **-ent** are related to *nouns* which end in **-ence**:

> *convalescent > convalescence*

## convenient

The "ee" sound after **v** is spelt with an **e**.
There is an **i** after the **n**.

A related word is
  noun **convenience**

☆ Remember: A le**nient** con**ven**t would be **convenient**.
☆ Or break this word down into smaller parts to help you remember the spelling:
  *con + ven + i + ent*

## coolly

There are two **l**s in **coolly**.

Coolly is made up of the *adjective* **cool** plus the *adverb suffix* **-ly** added at the end. When the suffix **-ly** is added to a word which ends in **l**, there will be two **l**s:
  *cool+ly = coolly*

## cord, chord

These two spellings are often confused.

**Cord** is strong thick string or electrical wire.
Your vocal **cords** are folds in your throat which are used to produce sound.
A **chord** is a group of three or more musical notes played together.

☆ Remember: A **chor**d is played in **chor**us.

## correspond

There is a double **r** in correspond.

Related words are
> noun **correspondence**
> noun **correspondent**

☆    Remember:    Don't    **corre**ct    my **corre**spondence.
☆ Or: There is a **dent** in the correspon**dent**.

## corridor

There is a double **r** in corridor.
The ending is **-or**.

☆ Remember: **Dor**is is in the corri**dor**.

## council, counsel

These words sound the same and they can be confused.

A **council** is a group of people elected to look after the affairs of an area.
**Counsel** is advice.
To **counsel** is to give advice.

Related·words are
> noun **councillor**
> noun **counsellor**

☆ Remember: The coun**cil** have pen**cils**.

## counterfeit
The end of counterfeit is **-eit**.

☆ Remember: If you counter**feit** it will **e**nd **i**n **t**ears.

## courageous
Courageous begins with **cou-**.
There is an **e** before the **-ous** ending.

RULE A final silent **E** is usually dropped when an ending which begins with a vowel is added. But this **E** is retained for the endings **-CE** or **-GE** when these letters keep a *soft* sound:

> *courage+ous* > *courageous*

RULE The "uss" sound at the end of an *adjective* is almost always spelt **-ous**.

## courteous
Courteous begins with **cou-**.
There is an **e** after the **t**.

RULE The "uss" sound at the end of an *adjective* is almost always spelt **-ous**.

A related word is
> noun **courtesy**

## crèche
This word came into English from French.
There is an *accent* above the **e**.

The "sh" sound is spelt **ch**.
There is an **e** at the end. The ending is **-che**.

☆ Remember: a **che**ap and **che**erful crè**che**

## crescent
The "ss" sound in crescent is spelt **sc**.

☆ Remember: There is a **scent** in the cre**scent**.

## criticize *or* criticise
The ending of this word is **-cize** or **-cise**.

Related words are
  *noun* **critic**
  *noun* **criticism**

☆ Remember that the words criticize and criticism are related to the word critic. The **c** at the end of criti**c** may help you to remember the letter **c** is also in criti**c**ize and criti**c**ism.

## crochet
The "sh" sound in crochet is spelt **ch**.
The ending is **-et**.

The different *verb* forms of crochet are:
  **crochets**
  **crocheting**
  **crocheted**

## crocodile

The middle part of crocodile is spelt **co**.

☆ Remember: Cro**cod**iles eat **cod**.

## crucial

The "oo" sound in crucial is spelt **u**. The beginning is **cru-**.
The "sh" sound is spelt **ci**.

☆ Remember: A spe**cial** offi**cial** commer**cial** is cru**cial**.

## cubicle

The vowel after **b** in cubicle is **i**.
The ending is **-cle**.

☆ Remember: Don't leave any art**icle**s in the cub**icle**s.

## cupful

There is one **l** at the end of cupful.

RULE The *suffix* **-FUL** is always spelt with one **L**.

## curiosity

There is no **u** before the **s** in curiosity, even though it is connected to the word **curious**.

☆ Remember how it is curious that curiosity has no **u** when curio**us** does.

## currant, current
These words sound the same and they can be confused.

A **currant** is a small dried grape.
A **current** is a flow of water, air, or electricity.
**Current** also means happening.

☆ Remember: There are curr**a**nts in c**a**kes and curr**e**nts in **e**lectricity.

## currency
There is a double **r** in currency.
There is an **e** before the **n**.

☆ Remember that something with currency is happening **currently** or is the **current** type of money used in a country.
☆ Or remember: C**en**ts and p**en**nies are curr**en**cy.

## curriculum
There is a double **r** and a single **c** in curriculum.

## curriculum vitae
This is a Latin term.
There is a double **r** and a single **c** in curriculum.
Vitae ends in **-ae**.

## curtains
The vowel sound after **t** in curtains is spelt **ai**.

☆ Remember: Cert**ai**n curt**ai**ns are pl**ai**n.

## cylinder

The "ss" sound in cylinder is spelt with the letter **c**.
The first vowel in cylinder is **y**. The beginning is
**cy-**.
The ending is **-er**.

## cynic

The "ss" sound in cynic is spelt with the letter **c**.
The vowel after the **c** is **y**. The beginning is **cy-**.
The final "k" sound is spelt with the letter **c** as
well.

A related word is
*adjective* **cynical**

The word is made up of the *noun* **cynic** plus the
*suffix* **-al** added at the end:
**cynic+al = cynical**

☆ Remember: **C**an't **Y**ou **N**ote **I**t **C**arefully?

# D

## dachshund
There is a **ch** followed by a **sh** in dachshund.

☆ Remember: **Da**chshunds **ch**ase **sh**eep through the **und**ergrowth.

## daffodil
There is a double **f** in daffodil.
This is followed by **o**.
The ending is **-dil**, with a single **l**.

☆ Break this word down into smaller parts to help you remember the spelling:

*daff + o + dil*

## dairy, diary
These two words are sometimes confused.

A **dairy** is a shop selling milk, cream, and cheese.
**Dairy** products are foods made from milk.
A **diary** is a small book in which you keep a record of appointments.

☆ Remember: the d**air**y next to the **air**port

# decease

The first "ss" sound is spelt with a single **c**.
The second "ss" sound is spelt with a single **s**.
The "ee" sound is spelt **ea**.

This word is made up of the *verb* **cease** with the *prefix* **de-** added at the beginning:

### de+cease = decease

This word, which means to die, can be confused with the word **disease**, an unhealthy condition.

A related word is
*adjective* **deceased**

☆ Remember that if you are de**ceased** you have **ceased** to be.

# deceive

The **e** comes before the **i** in deceive.

RULE I before E except after **c**, when they make the sound "ee".

# decide

Decide begins with **de-**.
The "ss" sound is spelt with a single **c**.

A related word is
*noun* **decision**

☆ Remember: a **de**liberate **de**cision

## decrease

The "ee" sound is spelt **ea**.
The "ss" sound is spelt with a single **s**.

☆ Remember: Decr**ease** with **ease**.

## definite

There is an **i** after the **f** in definite.
There is also an **i** after the **n**. The ending is **-ite**.

A related word is
  *adverb* **definitely**

Another related word is
  *noun* **definition**

☆ Remember that the words definite and definition are related to the word **define**. The "eye" sound of **define** may help you to remember that the letter after **f** in def**i**nite and def**i**nition is also **i**.

## defuse, diffuse

These two words are often confused.

To **defuse** something is to make it less dangerous or tense: *The King will try to defuse the crisis*; *Police defused a powerful bomb*.
To **diffuse** something is to spread it or cause it to scatter: *The message was diffused widely*; *curtains to diffuse the glare of the sun*.
**Diffuse** means spread over a wide area.

## deliberate

**Deliberate** begins with **de-**.
There is an **e** after the **b** which is sometimes missed out in speech.
The ending is **-ate**.

A related word is
*noun* **deliberation**

☆ If you remember the spelling of the word delib**era**tion, it may help you to remember that there is an **e** after the **b** in delib**era**te, and also an **-ate** ending.

☆ Or remember: a **de**liberate **de**cision

## delicious

**Delicious** starts with **de-**.
The "sh" sound is spelt **ci**.
The ending is **-cious**.

RULE The "uss" sound at the end of an *adjective* is almost always spelt **-ous**.

## demeanour

**Demeanour** begins with **de-**.

☆ Remember: De**meanour** can **mean our** behaviour.

## denunciation

There is no **o** before the **u** of denunciation, even though it is connected to the word **denounce**.

## deod<u>o</u>rant

Deodorant is made up of three parts:

   *de + odor + ant*

There is no **u** in this word, even though it is connected to the word **odour**.

## dependant, dependent

These two spellings are often confused.

**Dependant** is the *noun*: *The child is her dependant.*
**Dependent** is the *adjective*: *a dependent child.*

A related word is
   noun **dependence**

Dependence ends in **-ence**.

## derogat<u>o</u>ry

There is an **o** after the **t** in derogatory which is sometimes missed out in speech. The ending is **-ory**.

☆ Remember: deroga**tory** remarks about a **tory**

## de<u>sc</u>end

The "ss" sound in descend is spelt **sc**.
The opposite of descend is also spelt with **sc**:
   *a<u>sc</u>end*

A related word is
   noun **descent**

☆ Remember: De**sc**end by the **esc**alator.

## describe
**Describe** begins with **de-**.

A related word is
  noun **description**

## desert, dessert
These two words are often confused.

A **desert** is a region of land with little plant life.
To **desert** someone is to abandon them.
A **dessert** is sweet food served after the main course of a meal.

☆ Remember: A de**ss**ert is a **s**ticky **s**weet.

## desiccated
There is one **s** and two **c**s in **desiccated**.

☆ Remember that there is one **s** and two **c**s in de**sic**cated and one **s** and two **c**s in **c**o**c**onut**s** as well.

## desirable
Desirable begins with **de-**.
There is no **e** after the **r**.

RULE A final silent **E** is dropped when an ending which begins with a vowel is added:
  **desire+able > desir+able = desirable**

## desperate

There is an **e** after the **p** in **desperate**.
The ending is **-ate**.

A related word is
  *noun* **desperation**

☆ If you remember the spelling of the word
desperation, it may help you to remember that
there is an **e** after the **p** in desperate, and an **-ate**
ending.

## detach

Detach doesn't have a **t** at the end, just **-ch**.
The opposite of **detach** is also spelt with **-ch**:
  **attach**

## deter

The different *verb* forms of deter are:
  **deters**
  **deterred**
  **deterring**

A related word is
  *noun, adjective* **deterrent**

RULE When an ending which begins with a vowel
is added to a word which ends in a single vowel
plus a consonant, the consonant is doubled if the
*stress* is on the end of the word:
  **deter+ed > deterr+ed = deterred**
  **deter+ing > deterr+ing = deterring**

*deter+ent > deterr+ent = deterrent*

# develop

There is no **e** at the end of develop.

The different *verb* forms of develop are:
**develops**
**developed**
**developing**

RULE When an ending which begins with a vowel is added to a word which ends in a single vowel plus a consonant, the consonant is doubled if the *stress* is on the end of the word.

The stress in develop is not on the end of the word, therefore:
**develop+ed = developed**
**develop+ing = developing**

A related word is
*noun* **development**

# device, devise

These two spellings are often confused.

**Device**, with a **c**, is the *noun*: *a safety device.*
**Devise**, with an **s**, is the *verb*: *The schedule that you devise must be flexible.*

Other words where **-ice** is the *noun*, and **-ise** is the *verb* are:
*noun* **advice**

*verb* **advise**

*noun* **practice**

*verb* **practise**

☆ De**vice** contains the *noun* **ice**, while de**vise** contains the *verb* **is**.

## dialogue
The last two letters of dialogue are **-ue**. The ending is **-gue**.

*U.S. spelling (sometimes)*
   **dialog**

## diaphragm
The **f** sound in diaphragm is spelt **ph**.
There is a silent **g** before the **m**.

## diarrhoea
There is a double **r** in the word diarrhoea.
This double **r** is followed by an **h**.
The final three letters are **-oea**.

## diary, dairy
These two words are sometimes confused.

A **diary** is a small book in which you keep a record of appointments.
A **dairy** is a shop selling milk, cream, and cheese.

☆ Remember: **Dia**na's **dia**ry

## different

There is an **e** after the double **f** in different which is sometimes missed out in speech.

A related word is
*noun* **difference**

☆ If you remember that diff**e**rent and diff**e**rence are connected to the *verb* **differ** you will remember the **e**.

## diffuse, defuse

These two words are often confused.

To **diffuse** something is to spread it or cause it to scatter: *The message was diffused widely; curtains to diffuse the glare of the sun.*
**Diffuse** means spread over a wide area.
To **defuse** something is to make it less dangerous or tense: *The King will try to defuse the crisis; Police defused a powerful bomb.*

## dilapidated

The beginning of dilapidated is **di-**.

☆ Remember: a **di**sused **di**lapidated building

## dilemma

There is one **l** and two **m**s in dilemma.

☆ Remember: **Emma** is in a dil**emma**.

# dinosaur

The middle vowel in dinosaur is **o**.
The ending is **-aur**.

☆ Remember: There are **no** di**no**saurs now.

# disappear

There is one **s** and two **p**s in disappear.

The word is made up of the *verb* **appear** plus the *prefix* **dis-** added at the beginning, to make it mean the opposite:

  ***dis+appear = disappear***

☆ Remember: H**is** apple d**isapp**eared.

# disappoint

There is one **s** and two **p**s in disappoint.

Related words are
  *adjective* **disappointed**
  *noun* **disappointment**

☆ Remember: Th**is** apple is a d**isapp**ointment.

# disapprove

There is one **s** and two **p**s in disapprove.

A related word is
  *noun* **disapproval**

## disastrous

Remember that there is no **e** in disastrous, even though it is connected to the word **disaster**.

## disc, disk

These two spellings are often confused.

A **disc** is a flat round object.
A **disc** can be a piece of cartilage in your spine.
A **disc** can be a storage device used in computers, but the spelling **disk** is often preferred.

**Disk** is a chiefly American spelling of the above.

The name **compact disc** is always spelt with a **c**, even in American English.

## discipline

The "ss" sound in discipline is spelt **sc**.

☆ Remember: You need di**sci**pline to do **sci**ence.

## discreet, discrete

These two spellings are often confused.

If you are **discreet** you do not cause embarrassment with private matters.
**Discrete** things are separate or distinct.

☆ Remember that the **e**s in discr**e**t**e** (meaning separate) <u>are</u> separate.

## disease

The first "z" sound is spelt with a single **s**.
The second "z" sound is spelt with a single **s**.
The "ee" sound is spelt **ea**.

This word, which means an unhealthy condition, can be confused with the word **decease**, to die.

This word is made up of the word **ease** with the *prefix* **dis-** added at the beginning:
   *dis+ease = disease*

A related word is
   *adjective* **diseased**

## dispel

There is only one **l** at the end of dispel.

The different *verb* forms of dispel are:
   **dispels**
   **dispelling**
   **dispelled**

RULE When an ending which begins with a vowel is added to a word which ends in a single consonant plus **L**, the **L** is doubled:
   *dispel+ing > dispell+ing = dispelling*
   *dispel+ed > dispell+ed = dispelled*

## dissatisfy

There is a double **s** in di**ss**atisfy.

The word is made up of the *verb* **satisfy** plus the

*prefix* **dis-** added at the beginning, to make it mean the opposite. When the prefix **dis-** is added to a word which begins with **s**, there will be a double **s**:

   *dis+satisfy = dissatisfy*

## dissect

There is a double **s** in dissect, even though the beginning is sometimes pronounced "dise" rather than "diss".

## dissimilar

There is a double **s** in di**ss**imilar.

The word is made up of the *adjective* **similar** plus the *prefix* **dis-** added at the beginning, to make it mean the opposite. When the prefix **dis-** is added to a word which begins with **s**, there will be a double **s**:

   *dis+similar = dissimilar*

## distraught

There is a silent **gh** in distraught.

☆ Remember: You'll be distr**aught** if you get c**aught**.

## divisible

**Divisible** begins with **di-**.
The ending is **-ible**.

Related words are
    verb **divide**
    noun **division**

## don't

This is a shortened form of the words **do not**.
There is an *apostrophe* between the **n** and the **t**.

RULE In shortened forms of words or combinations of words with an *apostrophe*, the apostrophe appears in the place where a letter or letters have been missed out:

**do+not > do+nt > don+t = don't**

## doubt

There is a silent **b** before the **t** in doubt.

☆ Remember: **Doub**le-check if in **doub**t.

## draft, draught

These words sound the same and they can be confused.

A **draft** is an early rough version of a speech or document.
A **draught** is a current of cold air or an amount of liquid you swallow.
A place that is **draughty** has currents of cold air blowing through it.
**Draughts** is the game.
A person who draws plans is a **draughtsman**.

☆ Remember: A dr**aft** is **a f**irst **t**ry and a dra**ught** goes thro**ugh**.

## drunke<u>nn</u>ess

There are two **n**s in drunkenness.

The word is made up of the *adjective* **drunken** plus the *suffix* **-ness** added at the end. When the suffix **-ness** is added to a word which ends with **n**, there will be two **n**s:

*drunken+ness = drunkenness*

## dry

The spelling of words related to dry can be confusing.

Related words are
*adjective* **drier** or **dryer**
*adjective* **driest** or **dryest**

Other related words are
*noun* **dryer** or **drier**
*noun* **dryness**

The *noun* dryness is always spelt with a **y**, and never with an **i**.

## duly

There is no **e** after the **u** in duly.

## dutiful

Dutiful ends in one **l**.

The letter after **t** is **i**.

RULE The *suffix* **-FUL** is always spelt with one **L**.

RULE When an ending is added to a word that ends in a consonant plus **Y**, the **Y** changes to **I** (unless the ending added already begins with **I**):

**duty+ful > duti+ful = dutiful**

☆ Remember: **If** you are dut**i**ful you will only put one **l**.

## dwarf

The *plural* of dwarf is:

**dwarfs** *or* **dwarves**

# E

## earring
There are two **r**s in earring. It is made up of the word **ear** plus the word **ring**:
*ear+ring = earring*

## eccentric
There are two **c**s at the beginning of eccentric.

A related word is
*noun* **eccentricity**

Eccentricity is made up of the word **eccentric** plus the *noun suffix* **-ity** added at the end:
*eccentric+ity = eccentricity*

## echo
Echo ends in **o**.

The *plural* of echo is made by adding **-es**:
*echo+es = echoes*

## ecstasy
The "eks" sound in ecstasy is spelt **ecs**.
The ending is **-asy**.

## effect, affect

These two words are often confused.

An **effect** is a result something gives or an impression something makes: *discoveries which have a profound effect on medicine.*

To **affect** something is to influence or change it: *Tiredness affected his concentration.*

There are two **f**s in effect and affect.

☆ Remember: To **a**ffect something is to **a**lter it but an **e**ffect is the **e**nd result.

## efferve<u>sce</u>

There are two **f**s in effervesce.
The "ss" sound is spelt **sc**. The ending is **-sce**.

Related words are
   *adjective* **effervescent**
   *noun* **effervescence**

☆ Remember: Efferve**scent** ends in **scent**.

A number of *adjectives* which end in **-ent** are related to *nouns* which end in **-ence**:
   **effervescent** > **effervescence**

## efficient

There are two **f**s in efficient.
The "sh" sound is spelt **ci**.
The ending is **-cient**.

A related word is
*noun* **efficiency**

## eighth

There is only one **t** in eighth.
There is an **h** before and an **h** after this **t**.

☆ Remember: **E**dith **I**s **G**oing **H**ome **T**o **H**enry.

## elegant

The vowel after **l** in elegant is **e**.
The ending is **-ant**.

A related word is
*noun* **elegance**

☆ Remember: an e**leg**ant **leg**

## eligible

Eligible is spelt with one **l**.
The vowel after **l** is **i**.
The ending is **-ible**.

This word is sometimes confused with **illegible**.

**Eligible** means suitable to be chosen for something: *an eligible candidate*.
If something is **illegible** it is difficult to read: *illegible handwriting*.

☆ Eligible means suitable to be chosen, and so is related to the word **elect**, to choose. If you remember this, it might help you to remember that **e**ligible begins with **e**.

☆ Or remember: **El**ect someone **el**igible but think **ill** of their **ill**egible handwriting.

## elude, allude
These two words are often confused.

If something **eludes** you, you can't understand or remember it: *The name of the tune eludes me.*
If you **elude** something, you dodge or escape from it: *She managed to elude the police.*
To **allude** to something is to refer to it in an indirect way: *I never allude to an unpleasant matter.*

☆ Remember if something **e**ludes you it **e**scapes you.

## elusive, illusive
These two words are often confused.

Something **elusive** is difficult to find, describe, or remember: *an elusive name on the tip of the tongue.*
**Illusive** means the same as **illusory**. Something **illusive** seems to exist but doesn't really: *an illusive phantom.*

There is one **I** in elusive.
There are two **I**s in illusive.

☆ If you remember that elusive is connected to the word **elude** and that illusive is connected to the word **illusion**, it may help you to remember their spellings.

☆ Or remember that something **e**lusive **e**scapes you.

## emba<u>rr</u>a<u>ss</u>

There is a double **r** and a double **s** in **embarrass**.

Related words are
  adjective **embarrassed**
  adjective **embarrassing**
  noun **embarrassment**

All of these have a double **r** and a double **s**.

☆ Remember: If you are embarr**ass**ed you feel like an **ass**.

☆ Or: I was em**barr**assed to be **barr**ed.

## emphasize or emphasise

The "f" sound in emphasize is spelt **ph**.
The letter after **ph** is **a**.
The ending is **-size** or **-sise**.

A related word is
  noun **emphasis**

## encyclopedia or encyclopaedia

This word can be spelt with an **e** or an **ae** after **p**, although the form **encyclopedia** is more common.

## endeavour

The vowel sound after the **d** in endeavour is spelt **ea**.
The ending is **-our**.

## enquire *or* inquire

You can spell this word with an **e** or an **i**, although the form **inquire** is more common. Some people use the form **enquire** to mean "ask about", and the form **inquire** to mean "investigate".

A related word is
  *noun* **enquiry** *or* **inquiry**

## enrol

There is only one **l** at the end of enrol.

The different *verb* forms of enrol are:
  **enrols**
  **enrolling**
  **enrolled**

RULE  When an ending which begins with a vowel is added to a word which ends in a single consonant plus **L**, the **L** is doubled:
  **enrol+ing > enroll+ing = enrolling**
  **enrol+ed > enroll+ed = enrolled**

A related word is
  noun **enrolment**

A final **l** does not have to be doubled if the ending being added begins with a consonant.

## ensure, insure
These two words are often confused.

To **ensure** something happens is to make sure that it happens: *His performance ensured victory for his team.*
To **insure** something is to take out financial cover against its loss: *You can insure your cat or dog for a few pounds.*
To **insure** against something is to do something in order to prevent it or protect yourself from it: *Football clubs cannot insure against the cancellation of a match.*

A word related to **insure** is
  noun **insurance**

☆ Remember: **In**sur**ance** needs f**inance**.

## entirely
There is an **e** after the **r** in entirely.

The word is made up of the *adjective* **entire** plus the *adverb suffix* **-ly**:
  *entire + ly = entirely*

## envelop, envelope
These two words are often confused.

**Envelop** is the *verb* meaning to cover or surround.

**Envelope**, with an **e** at the end, is the *noun* meaning a paper covering which holds a letter.

The different *verb* forms of envelop are:
   *enveloped*
   *enveloping*

RULE When an ending which begins with a vowel is added to a word which ends in a single vowel plus a consonant, the consonant is doubled if the *stress* is on the end of the word.

The stress in envelop is not on the end of the word, therefore:
   *envelop+ed = enveloped*
   *envelop+ing = enveloping*

## environment
There is an **n** after the **o** in environment which is difficult to hear when the word is spoken.

☆ Remember: There is **iron** in the env**iron**ment.

## equal
There is one **l** at the end of equal.

The different *verb* forms of equal are:
   *equals*

> ### *equalling*
> ### *equalled*

**RULE** When an ending which begins with a vowel is added to a word which ends in a single vowel plus **L**, the **L** is doubled:

**equal+ing > equall+ing = equalling**
**equal+ed > equall+ed = equalled**

Another related word is
*verb* **equalize** or **equalise**

Equalize is an <u>exception</u> to the above rule, and the **l** is <u>not</u> doubled:

**equal+ize = equalize**

## equa**ll**y
There are two **l**s in equally.

The word is made up of the *adjective* **equal** plus the *adverb suffix* **-ly** added at the end. When the suffix **-ly** is added to a word which ends in **l**, there will be two **l**s:

**equal+ly = equally**

☆ Remember: **Ally** and S**ally** are equa**lly** pa**lly**.

## equip
The different *verb* forms of equip are:
> **equips**
> **equipping**
> **equipped**

RULE When an ending which begins with a vowel
is added to a word which ends in a single vowel
plus a consonant, the consonant is doubled if the
*stress* is on the end of the word:

   ***equip+ing* > *equipp+ing* = *equipping***
   ***equip+ed* > *equipp+ed* = *equipped***

Another related word is
   *noun* **equipment**

## erroneous
There are two **r**s in erroneous.
The ending is **-eous**.

☆ If you remember that erroneous is connected
to the word **error**, it may help you to remember
that there are two **r**s in err**r**oneous.

## especially
The "sh" sound in especially is spelt **ci**.
There are two **l**s at the end. The ending is **-ally**.

Especially is made up of the *adjective* **especial**
plus the *adverb suffix* **-ly** added at the end. When
the suffix **-ly** is added to a word which ends in **l**,
there will be two **l**s:

   ***especial+ly* = *especially***

## etc.
The **t** comes before the **c** in etc.
It should also be followed by a full stop.

☆ Etc. is an abbreviation for the Latin phrase **et cetera** which means "and the other (things)". If you remember this, it should remind you of the order of the letters, **et + c**.

## etiquette

There is one **t** at the beginning of etiquette.
The "k" sound is spelt **qu**.
There are two **t**s at the end of the word. The ending is **-ette**.

☆ Remember: The **Que**en uses eti**que**tte.

## euthanasia

Euthanasia starts with **eu-**.
The middle vowel is **a**.
The last part is **-asia**.

☆ Break this word down into smaller parts to help you remember the spelling:

   *eu + than + asia*

## exaggerate

There are two **g**s in exaggerate.
The vowel after **gg** is **e**.

A related word is
   *noun* **exaggeration**

☆ Remember: I am st**agger**ed by your ex**agger**ation.

### exasperate
The vowel after **p** is **e**. The middle part is **per**.

☆ Remember: **Per**haps I'm exas**per**ated.

### ex<u>ceed</u>
Exceed begins with **exc-**.
The ending is **-eed**.

A related word is
  adverb **exceedingly**

☆ Remember: I am exc**eed**ingly gr**eed**y.

### ex<u>cell</u>ent
Excellent begins with **exc-**.
There is a double **l** in the middle.
The ending is **-ant**.

RULE When an ending which begins with a vowel is added to a word which ends in a single vowel plus **L**, the **L** is doubled:
  **excel+ent > excell+ent = excellent**

☆ Remember: It is **excell**ent to **ex**it from a **cell**.

### except, accept
These two words are often confused.

**Except** means other than or apart from: I never wear a skirt except when we go out.
To **accept** something is to take or tolerate it: The King would not accept their demands.

☆ Remember that if you **exc**ept something you **exc**lude it.

## excerpt
Excerpt begins with **exc-**.
There is a silent **p** before the final **t**.

## excess
Excess begins with **exc-**.
There is a double **s** at the end. The ending is **-ess**.

The *plural* of excess is:
### excesses

RULE The *plural* of a word which ends in **s**, **x**, **z**, **sh**, or **ch** is made by adding **-es**:
### excess+es = excesses

Related words are
*adjective* **excessive**
*adverb* **excessively**

## excite
Excite begins with **exc-**.

Related words are
*adjective* **excited**
*adjective* **exciting**

RULE A final silent **e** is dropped when an ending which begins with a vowel is added:

*excite+ing > excit+ing = exciting*

Another related word is
  noun **excitement**

A final silent **e** may not be dropped when an ending which begins with a consonant is added:
  *excite+ment = excitement*

## exercise
The beginning of exercise is **exer-**.
There is no **c** until after the **r**.
The ending is **-ise**, and never **-ize**.

This word is sometimes confused with **exorcize**, meaning to get rid of an evil spirit.

☆ Remember: You exercise your legs but exorcize a ghost.

## exhaust
There is an **h** after the **ex-** in exhaust.

A related word is
  noun **exhaustion**

## exhibit
There is an **h** after the **ex-** in exhibit.

A related word is
  noun **exhibition**

☆ Remember: Exhibit exhibits an **h** after **x**.

## exhilarate

There is an **h** after the **ex-** in exhilarate.
The vowel after **l** is **a**.

A related word is
  noun **exhilaration**

## existence

The beginning of existence is **ex-**.
The ending is **-ence**.

The word is made up of the *verb* **exist** plus the *suffix* **-ence** added at the end:
  *exist+ence = existence*

## exorcize *or* exorcise

The beginning of exorcise (meaning to get rid of an evil spirit) is **exor-**.
There is a **c** after the **r**.
The ending is **-cize** or **-cise**.

This word can be confused with **exercise**.

☆ Remember: You ex**o**rcize a gh**o**st but ex**e**rcise your l**e**gs.

## expense

Expense ends in **-se**.

A related word is
  adjective **expensive**

## extension
Extension ends in **-sion**.

☆ If you remember that extension is related to the *adjective* **extensive**, it may help you to remember that there is an **s** in extension.

## extraordinary
There is an **a** in extraordinary which is sometimes missed out in speech.

The word is made up of two words:
  *extra+ordinary = extraordinary*

## extravagant
The vowel after **v** in extravagant is **a**.
The ending is **-ant**.

A related word is
  *noun* **extravagance**

☆ Remember: There are an extravagant number of **a**s in extra**v**a**g**ant.

## extrovert
The vowel after **tr-** in extrovert is **o**.

## facet̲ious
The "ss" sound in facetious is spelt **c**.
The "sh" sound is spelt **ti**.

RULE The "uss" sound at the end of an *adjective* is almost always spelt **-OUS**.

☆ Remember: A **fact** about **fac**etious is that it has all five vowels in alphabetical order.

## Fahr̲enheit
The beginning of Fahrenheit is spelt **Fah-**.
The end is spelt **-heit**.

☆ Break this word down into smaller parts to help you remember the spelling:
   *Fah + ren + heit*

## faithf̲ul
There is one **l** at the end of faithful.

RULE The *suffix* **-FUL** is always spelt with one **L**.

## famil̲iar
The end of familiar is **-iar**.

RULE When an ending is added to a word that ends in a consonant plus **Y**, the **Y** changes to **I** (unless the ending added already begins with **I**):

*family+ar > famili+ar = familiar*

Related words are
*noun **familiarity***
*verb **familiarize** or **familiarise***

## fam**i**ly

There is an **i** after the **m** of family which is sometimes missed out in speech.

☆ You are less likely to miss out the **i** in the middle of the word **family** if you remember its connection with the word **familiar**.

## fa**sc**inate

The "ss" sound in fascinate is spelt **sc**.

Related words are
*adjective **fascinated***
*adjective **fascinating***
*noun **fascination***

RULE A final silent **E** is dropped when an ending which begins with a vowel is added:

*fascinate+ed > fascinat+ed = fascinated*
*fascinate+ing > fascinat+ing = fascinating*
*fascinate+ion > fascinat+ion = fascination*

## fatigue
The ending of fatigue is **-gue**.

Related words are
*verb, adjective* **fatiguing**
*verb, adjective* **fatigued**

RULE A final silent **E** is dropped when an ending which begins with a vowel is added:
**fatigue+ing > fatigu+ing = fatiguing**
**fatigue+ed > fatigu+ed = fatigued**

## faun, fawn
These two words sound the same and they can be confused.

A **faun** is a legendary creature.
A **fawn** is a baby deer: *Bambi the fawn.*
**Fawn** is a pale brown colour.
To **fawn** on or over someone is to flatter them.

## favour
The ending of favour is **-our**.

Related words are
*adjective* **favourable**
*noun, adjective* **favourite**

The word favourite is made up of the word **favour** plus the *noun suffix* **-ite** added at the end:
**favour+ite = favourite**

☆ You are less likely to miss out the **ou** in

**favourite** if you remember that it is related to the
*noun* **favour**.
☆ Or remember: **our** fav**our**ite

*U.S. spellings*
   **favor**
   **favorable**
   **favorite**


# feas<u>ible</u>
The ending of feasible is **-ible**.

A related word is
   *noun* **feasibility**


# Feb<u>r</u>uary
There is an **r** after the **b** in February.


# f<u>eign</u>
There is a silent **g** in feign, before the **n**.
The "ay" sound is spelt **ei**, with the **e** before the **i**.
The ending is **-eign**.


# fero<u>ci</u>ous
The "sh" sound in ferocious is spelt **ci**.
The ending is **-cious**.

RULE The "uss" sound at the end of an *adjective* is
almost always spelt **-ous**.

## feud
The "yoo" sound in feud is spelt **eu**.

☆ Remember: **F**euds **E**nd **U**p **D**isastrously.

## fiancé, fiancée
These words came into English from French.
There is an *accent* above the **e**.

**Fiancé** is the *masculine* form of the word, used for a man: *Jemima's fiancé is called Jim.*
**Fiancée** is the *feminine* form of the word, used for a woman. It has an extra **e** at the end: *Jemima is Jim's fiancée.*

☆ Break this word down into smaller parts to help you remember the spelling:
  *fi + an + cé(e)*

## field
## fiend
## fierce
The **i** comes before the **e** in all the above words.

Rule **I** before **E** except after **C**, when they make the sound "ee".

## fifth
There is an **f** in fifth, before the **th**.

The **-ve** of **five** changes to **f** before the **-th** is added:

*five+th* > *fif+th* = *fifth*

A similar word is:
*twelve+th* > *twelf+th* = *twelfth*

# fight
Fight contains the silent letters **gh**. It has the pattern **-ight**.

☆ Remember: **F**rank **I**s **G**enerally **H**itting **T**ommy.

# final, finale
These two words are sometimes confused.

**Final** means last of a series.
A **final** is the last game or contest in a series to decide the winner: *the Scottish Cup Final.*
A **finale**, with an **e** at the end, is the finish of something, especially the last part of a piece of music or a show: *a fitting finale to the process; the finale of a James Bond film.*

# flair, flare
These two words sound the same and they can be confused.

**Flair** is ability: *She showed natural flair.*
A **flare** is a bright firework.
To **flare** is also to widen out: *flared trousers.*

## flammable
There are two **m**s in flammable.
The ending is **-able**.

A related word is
*noun* **flammability**

## fledgling *or* fledgeling
Fledgling *or* fledgeling can be spelt with or without an **e**, but the form **fledgling** is much more common.

## flour, flower
These two words sound the same and they can be confused.

**Flour** is used in baking.
A **flower** is part of a plant.

☆ Remember: Flo**ur** makes bisc**u**its and d**u**mplings.

## fluorescent
The first vowel sound in fluorescent is spelt **uo**.
The "ss" sound is spelt **sc**.

☆ Remember: Fluore**scent** ends in **scent**.

## focus
The different *verb* forms of this word can be spelt with or without a double **s**:
*focuses or focusses*

*focusing* or *focussing*
*focused* or *focussed*

The *plural* of **focus** is:
**focuses**

RULE The *plural* of a word which ends in **S**, **X**, **Z**, **SH**, or **CH** is made by adding **-ES**:
**focus+es = focuses**

## forcible
Forcible ends in **-ible**.

A related word is
*adverb* **forcibly**

## for<u>ei</u>gn
There is a silent **g** in foreign, before the **n**.
**ei** comes before the **g**. The ending is **-eign**.

A related word is
*noun* **foreigner**

The *noun* **foreigner** is made up of the *adjective* **foreign** plus the *noun suffix* **-er** added at the end:
**foreign+er = foreigner**

## forf<u>ei</u>t
The **e** comes before the **i** in forfeit.

## forgo

There is no **e** in **forgo**.

## fortunate

There is no **e** after the **n** in fortunate.

**RULE** A final silent **E** is dropped when an ending which begins with a vowel is added:

### *fortune+ate* > *fortun+ate* = *fortunate*

A related word is
*adverb* **fortunately**

**Fortunately** is made up of the *adjective* **fortunate** plus the *adverb suffix* **-ly** added at the end.
Although a final silent **e** is dropped when an ending which begins with a vowel is added, the final **e** may not be dropped when an ending which begins with a consonant is added:

### *fortunate+ly* = *fortunately*

☆ Remember: For**tunate**ly the **tuna** she **ate** was very good.

## forty

There is no **u** in forty.

## foul, fowl

These words sound the same and they are often confused.

**Foul** means dirty or unpleasant: *foul play*.
A **foul** is also an illegal challenge in a sport.
**Fowl** are certain types of birds which can be eaten.

☆ Remember: An **owl** is a f**owl** but foul is **u**npleasant.

## foy**er**

This is a word which came into English from French.

The ending is **-er**.

## frankin**c**en**s**e

The first "ss" sound is spelt with a single **c**.
The second "ss" sound is spelt with a single **s**.

The word is made up of the word **frank** plus the word **incense**:

   *frank+incense = frankincense*

## fr**ei**ght

The **e** comes before the **i** in freight.

☆ Remember: **eight** tonnes of fr**eight**
☆ Or remember this word as being spelt **fr** plus the word **eight**:

   *fr + eight = freight*

## fridge
There is a **d** in fridge, although the full form is **refrigerator**.

## friend
The **i** comes before the **e** in friend.

☆ Remember: Fri**end** ends in **end**.
☆ Or: My **frie**nd likes **frie**s.

## frighten<u>ed</u>
Frightened contains the silent letters **gh**.
The ending is **-ened**.

The word is made up of the *verb* **frighten** plus the *suffix* **-ed** added at the end.

☆ Break this word down into smaller parts to help you remember the spelling:
   *fright + en + ed*

## ful<u>fil</u>
Fulfil ends in one **l**. The ending is **-fil**.
There is one **l** in the first part. The beginning is **ful-**

Related words are
   *verb, adjective* **fulfilled**
   *verb, adjective* **fulfilling**

RULE When an ending which begins with a vowel

is added to a word which ends in a single vowel plus **L**, the **L** is doubled:

**fulfil+ed > fulfill+ed = fulfilled**
**fulfil+ing > fulfill+ing = fulfilling**

Another related word is
noun **fulfilment**

If the ending begins with a consonant, the **l** may not be doubled:

**fulfil+ment > fulfilment**

## fullness
There are two **l**s in fullness.

The word is made up of the *adjective* **full** plus the *noun suffix* **-ness** added at the end:

**full+ness = fullness**

## fundamental
The letter **a** comes after the word **fund** in fundamental.

☆ Break this word down into smaller parts to help you remember the spelling:

**fun + da + men + tal**

## furniture
The middle letter of furniture is **i**.
The "cher" sound is spelt **-ture**.

# G

## gallop

The different *verb* forms of gallop are:

**gallops**
**galloped**
**galloping**

RULE When an ending which begins with a vowel is added to a word which ends in a single vowel plus a consonant, the consonant is doubled if the *stress* is on the end of the word.

The stress in gallop is not on the end of the word, therefore:

**gallop+ed = galloped**
**gallop+ing = galloping**

## gas

The different *verb* forms of gas are:

**gases** or **gasses**
**gassing**
**gassed**

The *plural* is:

**gases** or **gasses**

A related word is

*adjective* **gaseous**

# gâ<u>teau</u> *or* gat<u>eau</u>

This is a word which came into English from French.

There is sometimes an *accent* above the **a**.

The "oh" sound is spelt **eau**.

RULE The *plural* of a word which ends in **-EAU** is made by adding **s** or **x**:

   ***gateaus** or **gateaux***

# ga<u>ug</u>e

The "ay" sound in gauge is spelt **au**.

☆ Remember: **G**reat **A**unt **U**na **g**rows **e**ggplants.

# gen<u>e</u>rate

The vowel between **n** and **r** in generate is **e**.

A related word is
   *noun* **generator**

# gently

There is no **e** before or after the **l** in gently.

RULE When the *adverb suffix* **-LY** is added to an *adjective* which ends in a consonant followed by **-LE**, the **-LE** is usually dropped:

   ***gentle+ly** > **gent+ly** = **gently***

### genuine
The vowel combination after **n** in genuine is **ui**.
The ending is **-ine**.

### ghastly
There is an **h** after **g** in ghastly. It begins with **gh**.

☆ Remember: **gh**astly **gh**osts and **gh**ouls

### ghetto
There is an **h** after **g** in ghetto. It begins with **gh**.

The *plural* of ghetto is:
   **ghettos** *or* **ghettoes**

### ghost
There is an **h** after **g** in ghost. It begins with **gh-**.

☆ Remember: **gh**astly **gh**osts and **gh**ouls

### ghoul
There is an **h** after **g** in ghoul. It begins with **gh-**.

A related word is
   *adjective* **ghoulish**

☆ Remember: **gh**astly **gh**osts and **gh**ouls

### gipsy *or* gypsy
This word can be spelt with an **i** or an **y**, but the

form **gypsy** is more common.

The *plural* is:
 **gipsies** *or* **gypsies**

RULE The *plural* of a word which ends in a consonant plus **y** is made by changing the **y** to **i** and adding **-ES** :
 **gipsy** > **gipsi+es = gipsies**

## giraffe
There is one **r** and two **f**s in giraffe.
The ending is **-ffe**.

## glam<u>our</u>
Glam<u>our</u> ends in **-our**.

A related word is
 *adjective* **glamorous**

There is no **u** before the **r** in glamorous.

RULE When the *adjective suffix* **-ous** is added to a word ending in **-our**, the **u** of the **-our** is dropped:
 **glamour+ous** > **glamor+ous = glamorous**

Another related word is
 *verb* **glamorize** *or* **glamorise**

There is no **u** in glamorize.

*U.S. spelling (sometimes)*
 **glamor**

## glimpse
There is a **p** after the **m** in glimpse.
The ending is **-pse**.

## gnat
## gnaw
## gnome
## gnu
These words begin with a silent letter **g**.

## gorgeous
The beginning of gorgeous is **gor-**.
There is an **e** before the **-ous** ending.

RULE A final silent **E** is usually dropped when an ending which begins with a vowel is added. But this **E** is retained for the endings **-CE** or **-GE** when these letters keep a *soft* sound:

### gorge+ous = gorgeous

RULE The "uss" sound at the end of an *adjective* is almost always spelt **-OUS**.

## gorilla, guerrilla *or* guerilla
These two words are often confused.

A **gorilla** is a large ape.
A **guerrilla** is a member of a small unofficial army fighting an official one.

There is one **r** and two **l**s in gorilla.

☆ Remember: King Kong was a giant go**r**illa.

## gossip
The different *verb* forms of gossip are:
> *gossips*
> *gossiped*
> *gossiping*

RULE When an ending which begins with a vowel is added to a word which ends in a single vowel plus a consonant, the consonant is doubled if the *stress* is on the end of the word.

The stress in gossip is not on the end of the word, therefore:
> *gossip+ed = gossiped*
> *gossip+ing = gossiping*

## gove<u>rn</u>ment
There is an **n** after the **r** in government.

This word is made up of the *verb* **govern** with the *suffix* **-ment** added at the end:
> *govern+ment = government*

A related word is
> noun **governor**

The ending of governor is **-or**.

## gra<u>ffi</u>ti
There are two **f**s and one **t** in graffiti.

## grammar

The ending of grammar is **-ar**.

A related word is
  adjective **grammatical**

☆ If you remember that the word grammar is connected to the word **grammatical**, it may help you to remember that the letter after the double **m** is **a**.

☆ Or remember: **Ar**e you using correct gramm**ar**?

## grandeur

The ending of grandeur is **-eur**.

## grateful

The "ay" sound in grateful is spelt **a**.
There is an **e** after the **t**.
It ends in one **l**.

RULE The *suffix* **-FUL** is always spelt with one **L**.

A related word is
  noun **gratitude**

☆ If you remember that the word grateful is connected to the word **gratitude**, it may help you to remember that the vowel after the **gr** is **a**.

☆ Or remember: You should be gr**ate**ful for what you **ate**.

## grey
The vowel in grey is **e**. It can also be spelt **gray**, but this is usually considered to be the U.S. spelling.

## grief
The **i** comes before the **e** in grief.

RULE **I** before **E** except after **C**, when they make the sound "ee".

Related words are
  verb **grieve**
  noun **grievance**
  adjective **grievous**

There is no **i** after the **v** in grievous.

RULE A final silent **E** is dropped when an ending which begins with a vowel is added:
  **grieve+ous > griev+ous = grievous**

## grisly, grizzly
These two words are often confused.

**Grisly** means nasty and horrible: *grisly murders*.
**Grizzly** means grey or streaked with grey: *a grizzly beard*.
A **grizzly** is also a type of bear.

## gruesome
There is an **e** after the **u** in gruesome.

## guarantee

Guarantee begins with **gu-**.

The vowel between **r** and **n** is **a**. The middle part is **ran**.

The ending is **-ee**.

The different *verb* parts of guarantee are:

> **guarantees**
> **guaranteeing**
> **guaranteed**

☆ Remember: The **gu**ard **gu**aranteed that the **gu**est was **gu**ilty.

☆ Or break this word down into smaller parts to help you remember the spelling:

> **gua + ran + tee**

## guard
## guess
## guest
## guide
## guillotine
## guilty
## guitar

All these words begin with **gu-**.

## guerrilla *or* guerilla, gorilla

These words can be confused.

A **guerrilla** is a member of a small unofficial army fighting an official one.

A **gorilla** is a large ape.

☆ Remember: King Kong was a giant gorilla.

You can spell guerrilla with one **r** or two, but the form **guerrilla** is more common.
Guerrilla always has a double **l**.

## guidance
Guidance begins with **gu-**.
There is no **e** after the **d**.

RULE A final silent **E** is dropped when a new ending which begins with a vowel is added:
 *guide+ance* > *guid+ance = guidance*

The ending is **-ance**.

## gullible
The ending of gullible is **-ible**.

## gymkhana
The "k" sound in gymkhana is spelt **kh**.

## gymnasium
Gymnasium begins with **g** followed by **y**. It is sometimes shortened to **gym**.

## gymnastics
Gymnastics begins with **g** followed by **y**. It starts with the word **gym**.

A related word is
   *noun* **gymnast**

## gypsy *or* gipsy
This word can be spelt with a **y** or an **i**, but the
form **gypsy** is more common.

The *plural* is:
   **gypsies** *or* **gipsies**

RULE The *plural* of a word which ends in a
consonant plus **y** is made by changing the **y** to **i**
and adding **-ES**:
   **gypsy** > **gypsi+es = gypsies**

# haemorrhage

Haemorrhage begins with **haemo-**.
There are two **r**s after the **o**.
There is a silent **h** before the ending **-age**.

☆ Break this word down into smaller parts to help
you remember the spelling:

*hae + mo + rr + hage*

# hallucination

There is a double **l** in hallucination.
The "ss" sound is spelt with a single **c**.

A related word is
*verb* **hallucinate**

# handicap

The different *verb* forms of handicap are:
**handicaps**
**handicapped**
**handicapping**

RULE Usually, when an ending which begins with a
vowel is added to a word which ends in a single

vowel plus a consonant, the consonant is doubled if the *stress* is on the end of the word.

However, handicap is an <u>exception</u> to this rule, and the final consonant <u>is</u> doubled:

**handicap+ed > handicapp+ed = handicapped**
**handicap+ing > handicapp+ing =**
**handicapping**

## handkerchief

There is a **d** in handkerchief which is often missed out in speech.
The ending is **-chief**, with the **i** coming before the **e**.

RULE **i** before **e** except after **c**, when they make the sound "ee".

☆ Break this word down into smaller parts to help you remember the spelling:
**hand + ker + chief**

## happen

The different *verb* forms of happen are:
**happens**
**happened**
**happening**

RULE When an ending which begins with a vowel is added to a word which ends in a single vowel plus a consonant, the consonant is doubled if the *stress* is on the end of the word.

The stress in happen is not on the end of the word, therefore:

**happen+ed = happened**
**happen+ing = happening**

## happiness

There are two **p**s and one **n** in happiness.

RULE When an ending is added to a word which ends in a consonant plus **y**, the **y** changes to **i** (unless the ending added already begins with **i**):

**happy+ness > happi+ness = happiness**

## harangue

The last two letters of harangue are **-ue**. The ending is **-ngue**.

## harass

There is one **r** and a double **s** in harass.

A related word is
  noun **harassment**

## hatred

There is no **e** after the **t** in hatred.

## hazard

There is one **z** in hazard.

# h<u>ea</u>rse
The vowel sound in hearse is spelt **ea**.
The ending is **-rse**.

☆ Remember: I didn't **hear** the **hear**se.

# height
The **e** comes before **i** in height.
The ending is **-ght**.

☆ Remember: **eight** feet in h**eight**
☆ It may also help you to remember that w**eight** and h**eight** are very similar.
☆ Or remember this word as being spelt **h** plus the word **eight**:
   *h+eight = height*

# heir, heiress
Heir begins with a silent **h**.
The vowel sound is spelt **ei**.

☆ Remember: The **H**appy **E**arl **I**s **R**ich.

# heredit<u>a</u>ry
There is an **a** between the **t** and **r** in hereditary which is sometimes missed out in speech. The ending is **-ary**.

# her<u>o</u>
Hero ends in **o**.

The *plural* of hero is made by adding **-es**:

*hero+es = heroes*

A related word is
*noun* **heroism**

## hid<u>e</u>ous
There is an **e** after the **d** in hideous. The ending is
**-eous**.

☆ Remember: **Hide hide**ous things.

## hiera<u>rc</u>hy
The **i** comes before the **e** in hierarchy.
There is an **r** in the ending **-archy**.

☆ Remember: a hier**archy** of **arch**ers

## hieroglyphics
The beginning of hieroglyphics is **hie-**.
The vowel after **r** is **o**.
The vowel after **gl** is **y**.

☆ Remember: **H**idden **I**n **E**gypt, **R**emaining
**O**bscure.
☆ Or break this word down into smaller parts to
help you remember the spelling:

*hie + ro + gly + phics*

## hind<u>ra</u>nce
There is no **e** between the **d** and **r** of hindrance,
even though it is connected to the word **hinder**.

## hoard, horde
These two words are often confused.

To **hoard** is to save things.
A **hoard** is also a store of things that have been saved: *a priceless hoard of modern paintings.*
A **horde** is a large group of people, animals, or insects: *a horde of press photographers.*

## holiday
There is one **l** in holiday.
The vowel after **l** is **i**.

## holocaust
The beginning of holocaust is **holo-**.
The vowel sound after **c** is spelt **au**.

## honest
Honest begins with a silent **h**.
There is only one **n**.

Related words are
noun ***honesty***
adverb ***honestly***

## honour
Honour begins with a silent **h**.
There is only one **n**.
The ending is **-our**.

A related word is

*adjective* **honorary**

There is no **u** before the **r** in honorary.

RULE When the *adjective suffix* **-ARY** is added to a word which ends in **-OUR**, the **U** of the **-OUR** is dropped:

   ***honour+ary* > *honor+ary = honorary***

Another related word is
   *adjective* **honourable**

RULE When the *adjective suffix* **-ABLE** is added to a word ending in **-OUR**, the **U** is <u>not</u> dropped from the **-OUR** ending.

☆ Remember: The hon**our** is **our**s.

*U.S. spellings*
   **honor**
   **honorable**

# hope

The different *verb* forms of hope are:
   **hopes**
   **hoping**
   **hoped**

RULE A final silent **E** is dropped when an ending which begins with a vowel is added:

   ***hope+ing* > *hop+ing = hoping***
   ***hope+ed* > *hop+ed = hoped***

## hopeful

There is an **e** in hopeful.

The word is made up of the *noun* **hope** plus the *suffix* **-ful** added at the end:

### *hope+ful = hopeful*

RULE The *suffix* **-FUL** is always spelt with one **L**.

## horoscope

The beginning of horoscope is **horo-**.

☆ Break this word down into smaller parts to help you remember the spelling:

### *ho + ro + scope*

## horrible

There is a double **r** in horrible.
There is a similar double **r** in:

### te**rr**ible

The ending is **-ible**.

## horror

There is a double **r** in horror.
There is a similar double **r** in:

### te**rr**or

A related word is
*verb* **horrify**
*adjective* **horrified**

RULE When an ending is added to a word which

ends in a consonant plus **y**, the **y** changes to **i** (unless the ending added already begins with **i**):

*horrify+ed* > *horrifi+ed = horrified*

## hum<u>o</u>rous

There is no **u** before the **r** in humorous.

RULE When the *adjective suffix* **-ous** is added to a word ending in **-our**, the **u** of the **-our** is dropped:

*humour+ous* > *humor+ous = humorous*

RULE The "uss" sound at the end of an *adjective* is almost always spelt **-ous**.

## Hung<u>a</u>ry

Hungary is spelt with a capital **H**.

RULE The name or names of a country or other area on the map begin with a capital letter.

The ending is **-ary**.

This name is sometimes confused with the word **hungry**.

A related word is
    *noun, adjective* **Hungarian**

☆ If you remember the spelling of Hung**a**rian, it may help you to remember that there is an **a** after the **g** in Hung**a**ry.
☆ Or remember: **Gary** is from Hun**gary**.

## hungry

The ending of hungry is **-gry**.

This word is sometimes confused with the name of the country, **Hungary**.

☆ Remember: I get an**gry** when I'm hun**gry**.

## hurricane

There is a double **r** in hurricane.
The vowel after **rr** is **i**.
The ending is **-ane**.

☆ Remember: A **hurricane hurri**ed through Costa **Rica**.

## hyacinth

The "eye" sound in hyacinth is spelt **y**. The beginning is **hya-**.
The "ss" sound is spelt with a **c**. The ending is **-cinth**.

## hygiene

The "eye" sound in hygiene is spelt **y**. The beginning is **hy-**.
The **i** comes before the **e** to make the "ee" sound.

RULE **i** before **E** except after **c**, when they make the sound "ee".

A related word is

*adjective* **hygienic**

RULE  A final silent **E** is dropped when an ending which begins with a vowel is added:

**hygiene+ic > hygien+ic = hygienic**

## hyphen
Hyphen begins with **hy-**.
The "f" sound is spelt **ph**.
The ending is **-en**.

## hypochondriac
Hypochondriac begins with **hy-**.
The part which follows is spelt **po**. The whole first part is spelt **hypo-**.
The "k" sound is spelt **ch**.

☆ Remember: A **hypo**chondriac **hypo**crite gets **hy**sterical.

## hypocrisy
Hypocrisy begins with **hy-**.
The ending is **-isy**.

Related words include
  *noun* **hypocrite**
  *adjective* **hypocritical**

The vowel after **p** in the above words is also **o**. The beginning is **hypo-**.

☆ If you remember the spelling of hypocrite and

hypocritical, it may help you to remember that there is an **i** at the end of hypocri**s**y.

☆ If you remember the spelling of hyp**o**crisy, where the **o** is emphasized, it may help you to remember that there is an **o** in hyp**o**crite and hyp**o**critical.

☆ Or remember: A **hypo**chondriac **hypo**crite gets **hy**sterical.

## hysteria

Hysteria begins with **hy-**.

Related words are
  *adjective* **hysterical**
  *adverb* **hysterically**

☆ Remember: W**hy** are you so **hy**sterical?

**idiosyncrasy**
The middle section is spelt **syn**.
The ending is **-asy**.

**idle, idol**
These two words sound the same and they are often confused.

An **idol** is a famous person worshipped by fans.
An **idol** is also a picture or statue worshipped as a god.
**Idle** means doing nothing.

☆ Remember: To id**le** takes **l**ittle **e**nergy.

A word related to idol is
  verb **idolize** or **idolise**

Words related to idle are
  noun **idleness**
  adverb **idly**

RULE When the *adverb suffix* **-LY** is added to an *adjective* which ends in a consonant followed by **-LE**, the **-LE** is usually dropped:
  *idle+ly > id+ly = idly*

## illegal

This word is made up of the *adjective* **legal** plus the *prefix* **il-** added at the beginning. When the prefix **il-** is added to a word beginning with **l**, there will be two **l**s:

**il+legal = illegal**

☆ Remember: To be **ill** is not **ill**egal.

## illegible

This word is made up of the *adjective* **legible** plus the *prefix* **il-** added at the beginning. When the prefix **il-** is added to a word beginning with **l**, there will be two **l**s:

**il+legible = illegible**

The ending is **-ible**.

The words **illegible** and **eligible** are sometimes confused.

If something is difficult to read it is **illegible**: *illegible handwriting.*
**Eligible** means suitable to be chosen for something: *an eligible candidate.*

☆ **El**igible means suitable to be chosen, and so is related to the word **el**ect, to choose. If you remember this, it might help you to remember that **e**ligible begins with **e**, whereas **i**llegible begins with **i**.

# illegitimate

This word is made up of the *adjective* **legitimate** plus the *prefix* **il-** added at the beginning. When the prefix **il-** is added to a word beginning with **l**, there will be two **l**s:

   *il+legitimate = illegitimate*

# illiterate

There is a double **l** in illiterate.
There is one **t** in the middle.
The ending is **-ate**.

This word is made up of the *adjective* **literate** plus the *prefix* **il-** added at the beginning. When the prefix **il-** is added to a word beginning with **l**, there will be two **l**s:

   *il+literate = illiterate*

# illusive, elusive

These two words are often confused.

Something **illusive** seems to exist but doesn't really. It is a fairly rare word which means the same as **illusory**: *an illusive phantom.*
Something **elusive** is difficult to find, describe, or remember: *an elusive name on the tip of the tongue.*

☆ Remember that **ill**usive is connected to the word **ill**usion, meaning something you think you can see but which does not really exist, and that

**el**usive is connected to the word **el**ude, meaning to escape or to defy memory or description. This may help you not to confuse their spellings.

## imagin<u>ary</u>

The ending of imaginary is **-ary**.

A related word is
  *adjective* **imaginative**

RULE A final silent **E** is dropped when an ending which begins with a vowel is added:
  *imagine+ary > imagin+ary = imaginary*
  *imagine+ative > imagin+ative = imaginative*

☆ If you remember that imaginary and imaginative are connected to the word **imagination**, where the **a** is more pronounced, it may help you to remember that there is an **a** after the **n** in imagin**a**ry and imagin**a**tive.

## im<u>i</u>tate

There is one **m** in imitate.
The vowel after **m** is **i**. The beginning is **imi-**.

A related word is
  *noun* **imitation**

## imm<u>e</u>diate

There are two **m**s in immediate.
The ending is **-iate**.

A related word is
  adverb **immediately**

## immoral
There are two **m**s in immoral.

This word is made up of the *adjective* **moral** plus
the *prefix* **im-** added at the beginning. When the
prefix **im-** is added to a word beginning with **m**,
there will be two **m**s:
  *im+moral = immoral*

## imprisoned
There is an **m** in imprisoned.

This word is made up of the word **prison** plus the
*prefix* **im-** added at the beginning, and the *suffix*
**-ed** added at the end:
  *im+prison+ed = imprisoned*

## impromptu
There is an **m** at the beginning of impromptu. The
beginning is **im-**.
The ending is **-u**.

☆ Break this word down into smaller parts to help
you remember the spelling:
  *im + prompt + u*

## inaccurate
This word is made up of the *adjective* **accurate**

plus the *prefix* **in-** added at the beginning:
  *in+accurate = inaccurate*

There are two **c**s in inaccurate, as in **accurate**.
The ending is **-ate**.

A related word is
  noun **inaccuracy**

# inadvertent
Inadvertent ends in **-ent**.

A related word is
  adverb **inadvertently**

# incense
The first "ss" sound in incense is spelt with a single **c**.
The second "ss" sound is spelt with a single **s**.

# incident
The "ss" sound in incident is spelt with a single **c**.
The vowel which follows is **i**.
The ending is **-ent**.

Related words are
  adjective **incidental**
  adverb **incidentally**

There is an **a** after the **t** in incidentally which is sometimes missed out in speech.

Incidental is made up of the *adjective* **incidental**

plus the *adverb suffix* **-ly** added at the end. When
the suffix **-ly** is added to a word which ends in **l**,
there will be two **l**s:

   *incidental+ly = incidentally*

## inconceivable
The **e** comes before the **i** in inconceivable.

RULE **i** before **e** except after **c**, when they make
the sound "ee".

RULE A final silent **e** is dropped when an ending
which begins with a vowel is added:

   *inconceive+able > inconceiv+able =
   inconceivable*

## incongruous
There is a **u** after the **gr** in incongruous. The
ending is **-uous**.

RULE The "uss" sound at the end of an *adjective* is
almost always spelt **-ous**.

☆ Break this word down into smaller parts to help
you remember the spelling:

   *in + con + gru + ous*

## increase
The "ee" sound is spelt **ea**.
The "ss" sound is spelt with a single **s**.

☆ Remember: Incr**ease** with **ease**.

## independent

Independent ends in **-ent**.

Unlike **dependent** and **dependant**, there is only one spelling for the *noun* and *adjective*, which is **independent**.

A related word is
  noun **independence**

☆ Remember: an independ**ent** mom**ent**

## indict

Indict, meaning to charge with a crime, is spelt very differently from the way it sounds (in-**dite**). The ending is **-ict**.

Another related word is
  noun **indictment**

There is a word **indite**, meaning to write or to dictate, but this is rarely used.

☆ Remember: **I N**ever **D**abble **I**n **C**riminal **T**hings.

## indifference

There is an **e** after the **ff** in indifference which is sometimes missed out in speech.

A related word is
  adjective **indifferent**

# indignant

The **g** comes before the **n** in indignant.
The ending is **-ant**.

☆ Break this word down into smaller parts to help you remember the spelling:

*in + dig + nant*

# indispens<u>able</u>

The ending of indispensable is **-able**.

# ineligible

Ineligible is spelt with one **n** and one **l**.
The vowel after **l** is **i**.
The ending is **-ible**.

The word is made up of the *adjective* **eligible** plus the *prefix* **in-** added at the beginning:

*in+eligible = ineligible*

# infall<u>ible</u>

Infallible has a double **l**.
The ending is **-ible**.

A related word is
  noun **infallibility**

# infer

The different *verb* forms of infer are:
  *infers*
  *inferring*

### *inferred*

RULE When an ending which begins with a vowel is added to a word which ends in a single vowel plus a consonant, the consonant is doubled if the *stress* is on the end of the word:

**infer+ing** > **inferr+ing** = **inferring**
**infer+ed** > **inferr+ed** = **inferred**

A related word is
*noun* **inference**

RULE If an ending which begins with a vowel is added to a word which ends in a single vowel plus a consonant and the stress moves from the end to the beginning of a word, the final consonant may not be doubled:

**infer+ence** = **inference**

## ingredient
The "ee" sound in ingredient is spelt **e**.
The ending is **-ient**.

## initial
The "sh" sound in initial is spelt **ti**.

A related word is
*adverb* **initially**

## initiate
The "sh" sound in initiate is spelt **ti**.

Related words are
　　*noun* **initiation**
　　*noun* **initiative**

## innocent
There is a double **n** in innocent.

A related word is
　　*noun* **innocence**

## innocuous
There are two **n**s and one **c** in innocuous. The beginning is **inn-**.

RULE The "uss" sound at the end of an *adjective* is almost always spelt **-ous**.

## inoculate
There is only one **n** and one **c** in inoculate.

A related word is
　　*noun* **inoculation**

## inquire *or* enquire
You can spell this word with an **i** or an **e**, although the form **inquire** is more common. Some people use the form **enquire** to mean "ask about", and the form **inquire** to mean "investigate".

A related word is
　　*noun* **inquiry** *or* **enquiry**

### inseparable
The letter after **p** in inseparable is **a**. The middle section is spelt **par**.
The ending is **-able**.

### install *or* instal
This word can be spelt with one **l** or two, although the form **install** is more common.

A related word is
  *noun* **instalment**

*U.S. spelling*
  **installment**

### insure, ensure
These two words are often confused.

To **insure** something is to take out financial cover against its loss: *You can insure your cat or dog for a few pounds.*
To **insure** against something is to do something in order to prevent it or protect yourself from it: *Football clubs cannot insure against the cancellation of a match.*
To **ensure** something happens is to make sure that it happens: *His performance ensured victory for his team.*

### integrate
The middle vowel sound in integrate is spelt **e**.

Related words are
 *adjective* **integral**
 *noun* **integrity**

☆ If you remember the spelling of the *noun* **integrity**, where the **e** is more pronounced, it may help you to remember that there is an **e** in int**e**gral.

## intelligence
There are two **l**s in intelligence.
The vowel after the double **l** is **i**.
The ending is **-ence**.

A related word is
 *adjective* **intelligent**

☆ Remember: I can **tell** the **gent** is in**tell**i**gent**.

## interest
There is an **e** after the first **t** of interest which is sometimes missed out in speech.

Related words are
 *verb, adjective* **interested**
 *verb, adjective* **interesting**

## interfere
There is an **r** before the **f** in interfere. The beginning is **inter-**.

A related word is

*noun* **interference**

## interrogate
There are two **r**s in interrogate.

Related words are
 *noun* **interrogation**
 *noun* **interrogator**

☆ Remember: In**terro**gation causes **terro**r.

## interrupt
There are two **r**s in interrupt.

A related word is
 *noun* **interruption**

☆ Remember: It is **terr**ible to in**terr**upt.

## intricate
The vowel between **r** and **c** in intricate is **i**.
The ending is **-ate**.

A related word is
 *noun* **intricacy**

☆ Remember: an in**tric**ate and accur**ate** mag**ic tric**k

## intrigue
The ending of intrigue is **-gue**.

Related words are

*verb, adjective* **intrigued**
*verb, adjective* **intriguing**

RULE A final silent **E** is dropped when an ending which begins with a vowel is added:
**intrigue+ed** > **intrigu+ed = intrigued**
**intrigue+ing** > **intrigu+ing = intriguing**

## introduce
Introduce begins with **intro-**.

A related word is
*noun* **introduction**

☆ Remember that the shortened form of the word introduction is **intro**.

## invisible
Invisible ends in **-ible**.

A related word is
*noun* **invisibility**

☆ Break these words down into smaller parts to help you remember the spellings:
**in + vi + si + ble**
**in + vi + si + bi + li + ty**

## involvement
There is an **e** after the **v** in involvement.

RULE A final silent **E** is dropped when an ending which begins with a vowel is added, but may not be dropped when an ending which begins with a consonant is added:

**involve+ment = involvement**

## irascible
The "ss" sound in irascible is spelt **sc**.
The ending is **-ible**.

A related word is
*noun* **irascibility**

## irrational
This word is made up of the *adjective* **rational** plus the *prefix* **ir-** added at the beginning. When the prefix **ir-** is added to a word beginning with **r**, there will be two **r**s:

**ir+rational = irrational**

## irregular
This word is made up of the *adjective* **regular** plus the *prefix* **ir-** added at the beginning. When the prefix **ir-** is added to a word beginning with **r**, there will be two **r**s:

**ir+regular = irregular**

## irrelevant
There is a double **r** in **irrelevant**.
The ending is **-ant**.

This word is made up of the *adjective* **relevant** plus the *prefix* **ir-** added at the beginning. When the prefix **ir-** is added to a word beginning with **r**, there will be two **r**s:

   *ir + relevant = irrelevant*

## irreplaceable

There is an **e** before the **-able** ending in irreplaceable.

RULE A final silent **E** is usually dropped when an ending which begins with a vowel is added. But this **E** is retained for the endings **-CE** or **-GE** when these letters keep a *soft* sound:

   *replace+able > replaceable*

There is a double **r** in **irreplaceable**.

The word is made up of the *adjective* **replaceable** plus the *prefix* **ir-** added at the beginning, and the *suffix* **-able** added at the end. When the prefix **ir-** is added to a word beginning with **r**, there will be two **r**s:

   *ir + replaceable = irreplaceable*

## irresistible

There is a double **r** in irresistible.
The ending is **-ible**.

This word is made up of the *adjective* **resistible** plus the *prefix* **ir-** added at the beginning. When the prefix **ir-** is added to a word beginning with **r**, there will be two **r**s:

   *ir + resistible = irresistible*

## irresponsible
There is a double **r** in **irresponsible**.
The ending is **-ible**.

This word is made up of the *adjective*
**responsible** plus the *prefix* **ir-** added at the
beginning. When the prefix **ir-** is added to a word
beginning with **r**, there will be two **r**s:

   ***ir+responsible = irresponsible***

A related word is
   *noun* ***irresponsibility***

RULE An *adjective* ending in **-IBLE** will form a *noun*
spelt **-IBILITY**, and an *adjective* ending in **-ABLE** will
form a *noun* spelt **-ABILITY**.

## irritable
There are two **r**s in irritable.
The second vowel, after the double **r**, is **i**.
The ending is **-able**.

Related words are
   *verb* ***irritate***
   *noun* ***irritation***

RULE A *verb* ending in **-ATE** will form an *adjective*
spelt **-ABLE**:
   ***irritate > irritable***

## itinerary
There is an **a** after the first **r** in itinerary which is

sometimes missed out in speech.

## its, it's

These two spellings are often confused.

**It's**, with an *apostrophe*, is a shortened form of **it is**. The apostrophe replaces the missing letter **i**: *It's cold.*

**Its**, without an *apostrophe*, is used when you are referring to something belonging or relating to things that have already been mentioned: *The lion lifted its head.*

RULE In shortened forms of words or combinations of words with an *apostrophe*, the apostrophe appears in the place where a letter or letters have been missed out:

*it+is > it+s = it's*

**J**

## jackal
Jackal ends in **-al**.

## jealous
The beginning of jealous is **jea-**.
The ending is **-ous**.

RULE The "uss" sound at the end of an *adjective* is almost always spelt **-ous**.

A related word is
noun ***jealousy***

☆ Remember: To be j**eal**ous isn't h**eal**thy.

## jeopardize *or* jeopardise
The beginning of jeopardize is **jeo-**.
The middle part is **par**.

☆ Remember: You could j**eopard**ize your safety with a l**eopard**.

## jersey
The ending of jersey is **-ey**.

The *plural* of jersey is:

*jerseys*

RULE The *plural* of a word which ends in a vowel plus **Y** is made by adding **-s**:
  *jersey+s = jerseys*

## jewel
The "oo" sound in jewel is spelt **ew**.
The ending is **-el**.

Related words are
  noun *jeweller*
  noun *jewellery*

There are two **l**s in jeweller and jewellery.

RULE When an ending which begins with a vowel is added to a word which ends in a single vowel plus **L**, the **L** is doubled:
  *jewel+er > jewell+er = jeweller*
  *jewel+ery > jewell+ery = jewellery*

There is an **e** after the double **l** in jewellery that is sometimes missed out in speech. The ending is **-ery**.

*U.S. spellings*
  *jeweler*
  *jewelry*

## jockey
The *plural* of jockey is:
  *jockeys*

RULE The *plural* of a word which ends in a vowel plus **y** is made by adding **-s**:

*jockey+s = jockeys*

## jodhpurs
There is an **h** after the **d** in jodhpurs.

☆ Remember: You wear jod**h**purs when you ride a **h**orse.

## journey
Journey begins with **jou-**.
The ending is **-ey**.
The *plural* of journey is:

*journeys*

RULE The *plural* of a word which ends in a vowel plus **y** is made by adding **-s**:

*journey+s = journeys*

☆ Remember: How was y**our** j**our**ney?

## judgment *or* judgement
This word can be spelt with or without an **e**, but the form **judgment** is more common.

### karat<u>e</u>
Karate ends in an **e**.

☆ Break this word down into smaller parts to help you remember the spelling:
*ka + ra + te*

### kee<u>nn</u>ess
There are two **n**s in keenness.

This word is made up of the *adjective* **keen** plus the *noun suffix* **-ness** added at the end. When the suffix **-ness** is added to a word which ends with **n**, there will be two **n**s:
*keen+ness = keenness*

### khaki
Khaki begins with **kh-**.
It ends in **-ki**.

### kidnap
The different *verb* forms of kidnap are:
*kidnaps*
*kidnapped*
*kidnapping*

Related words are
*noun* **kidnapping**
*noun* **kidnapper**

RULE When an ending which begins with a vowel
is added to a word which ends in a single vowel
plus a consonant, the consonant is doubled if the
*stress* is on the end of the word.

The stress in kidnap is not on the end of the word,
but the final consonant is still doubled:
*kidnap+ed* > *kidnapp+ed = kidnapped*
*kidnap+ing* > *kidnapp+ing = kidnapping*
*kidnap+er* > *kidnapp+er = kidnapper*

## kid<u>ney</u>
The ending of kidney is **-ey**.

The *plural* of kidney is:
**kidneys**

RULE The *plural* of a word which ends in a vowel
plus **y** is made by adding **-s**:
*kidney+s = kidneys*

<u>k</u>nackered
<u>k</u>nee
<u>k</u>neel
<u>k</u>nickers
<u>k</u>night
<u>k</u>nit
<u>k</u>not

**knock**
**know**
**knuckle**
All the above words begin with a silent **k**.

☆ Remember: I **kn**ow I'm too **kn**ackered to take the **kn**ots from my **kn**itting.

**knife**
The *plural* of knife is:
   ***knives***

**knowledge**
The ending of knowledge is **-dge**.

A related word is
   *adjective* ***knowledgeable***

RULE A final silent **E** is usually dropped when an ending which begins with a vowel is added. But this **E** is retained for the endings **-CE** or **-GE** when these letters keep a *soft* sound:
   ***knowledge+able*** > ***knowledgeable***

**label**
There is only one **l** at the end of label.

The different *verb* forms of label are:
*labels*
*labelling*
*labelled*

RULE When an ending which begins with a vowel is added to a word which ends in a single vowel plus **l**, the **l** is doubled:
*label+ed > labell+ed = labelled*
*label+ing > labell+ing = labelling*

**laboratory**
There is an **o** after **b** in laboratory which is sometimes missed out in speech.
The ending is **-ory**.

☆ Remember: There is a **rat** in the labo**rat**ory.

**labyrinth**
The vowel between **b** and **r** in labyrinth is **y**.

## lackadaisical

The first "k" sound in lackadaisical is spelt **ck**. The beginning is **lack-**.
The vowel after **ck** is **a**.
The "ay" sound is spelt **ai**.

☆ Remember: If you **lack a dai**ly paper then you are **lackadai**sical.
☆ Or break this word down into smaller parts to help you remember the spelling:

*lack + a + dai + si + cal*

## lacquer

The middle part of lacquer is spelt **cqu**.

☆ Break this word down into two parts to help you remember the spelling:

*lac + quer*

## language

The "gw" sound in language is spelt **gu**.
The ending is **-age**.

Related words are
*noun **linguist***
*adjective **linguistic***

## languor

The ending of languor is **-uor**. The **u** comes before the **o**.

A related word is

*adjective* **languorous**

Languorous is made up of the *noun* **languor** plus the *adjective suffix* **-ous**:

**languor+ous = languorous**

# larynx
There is a **y** in larynx. The ending is **-ynx**.

A related word is
   *noun* **laryngitis**

The vowel after **r** in laryngitis is **y**.
The **x** of larynx changes to **g** to give the "dj" sound.

☆ If you remember that **laryngitis** is a disease of the **larynx**, it may help you to remember that the vowel after **r** is **y**.

# lasagne
The ending of lasagne is **-gne**.

☆ Remember: **Agnes** thinks las**agne** and champ**agne** go together.

# laugh
Laugh has the combination of letters **-augh**.

A related word is
   *noun* **laughter**

## laundry

There is no **e** in laundry, even though it is related to the *verb* **launder**.

☆ Remember: Wash and **dry** at the laun**dry**.

## lay

The different *verb* parts of lay are:
*lays*
*laying*
*laid*

## lead, led

These two words when they sound the same are often confused.

**Lead**, when it is pronounced like "led", is a soft metal, or the part of a pencil that makes a mark: *lead poisoning*.
**Led** is the *past tense* of **lead**: *the road which led to the house*.

## league

The "ee" sound in league is spelt **ea**.
The ending is **-gue**.

## leant, lent

These two words sound the same and are often confused.

**Leant** is the *past tense* of **lean**: *She leant back in*

*her chair.*
**Lent** is the *past tense* of **lend**: *She was lent Maureen's spare wellingtons.*

## lecherous
There is no **t** in lecherous, just **ch**.
The ending is **-ous**.

RULE The "uss" sound at the end of an *adjective* is almost always spelt **-ous**.

## legible
There is no **d** in legible. The "dj" sound is made by **g** only.
The ending is **-ible**.

A related word is
 *noun* **legibility**

RULE An *adjective* ending in **-IBLE** will form a *noun* spelt **-IBILITY**, and an *adjective* ending in **-ABLE** will form a *noun* spelt **-ABILITY**:
 *legible* > *legibility*

## legitimate
Legitimate begins with **leg-**.
The vowel after **g** is **i**.
The ending is **-ate**.

## leisure
The **e** comes before **i** in leisure, which rhymes

with "measure".
The ending is **-sure**.

## length
There is a **g** after the **n** in length.
Another word like this is:
### strength

A related word is
*adjective* **lengthy**

☆ Remember that length is connected to the *adjective* lo**ng**, and it may help you to remember the **g**.

## leopard
Leopard begins with **leo-**.
The ending is **-ard**.

☆ Remember: A l**eopard** could put you in j**eopard**y.
☆ Or: **Leo** the **leo**pard.

## level
The different *verb* forms of level are:
### levels
### levelling
### levelled

RULE When an ending which begins with a vowel is added to a word which ends in a single vowel plus **L**, the **L** is doubled:

> *level+ed* > *levell+ed* = *levelled*
> *level+ing* > *levell+ing* = *levelling*

## liaise

There are two **i**s in liaise, one before and one after the **a**.

A related word is
   *noun* **liaison**

## library

There is an **a** after the first **r** in library which is sometimes missed out in speech.

A related word is
   *noun* **librarian**

RULE When an ending is added to a word that ends in a consonant plus **y**, the **y** changes to **i** (unless the ending added already begins with **i**):
   *library+an* > *librari+an* = *librarian*

☆ If you remember the spelling of the *noun* librarian, where the **a** is more pronounced, it may help you to remember that there is an **a** in library.

## licence, license

These two spellings are often confused.

**Licence**, ending in **-ce**, is the *noun*: *a driver's licence*; *a TV licence*.

**License**, ending in **-se**, is the *verb*: *Censors agreed to license the film; They were licensed to operate for three years.*

Other words where **-ce** is the *noun*, and **-se** is the *verb* are:

noun **advi<u>ce</u>**
verb **advi<u>se</u>**
noun **devi<u>ce</u>**
verb **devi<u>se</u>**
noun **practi<u>ce</u>**
verb **practi<u>se</u>**

☆ Remember that licen**ce** and licen**se** have the same endings as advi**ce** and advi**se**: **-ce** for the noun, **-se** for the verb.
☆ Or remember: i**ce** and licen**ce** are *nouns*, while licen**se** and i**s** are *verbs*.

## lieutenant
The beginning of lieutenant is spelt **lieu-**.

## life
The *plural* of life is:
   **lives**

## lightening, lightning
These two spellings are often confused.

**Lightening** is a form of the *verb* **lighten**, and

means "becoming lighter": *The sky was lightening*.
**Lightning**, without an **e**, is bright flashes of light
in the sky: *forked lightning*.

## limit
There is one **m** and one **t** in limit.

The different *verb* forms of limit are:
   *limits*
   *limited*
   *limiting*

RULE When an ending which begins with a vowel
is added to a word which ends in a single vowel
plus a consonant, the consonant is doubled if the
*stress* is on the end of the word.

The stress in limit is not on the end of the word,
therefore:
   *limit+ed = limited*
   *limit+ing = limiting*

## liquefy
The vowel after **qu** in liquefy is **e**, not **i**.

## liqueur
There is a **qu** in the middle of liqueur.
The ending is **-eur**.

## literature
There is one **t** at the beginning of literature.
There is an **e** after the **t** which is sometimes missed out in speech.
There is one **t** at the end.
The ending is **-ture**.

A related word is
 *adjective* **literate**
 *adjective* **literary**

Literate ends in **-ate**.

## litre
Litre ends in **-tre**.

*U.S. spelling*
 **liter**

## loath *or* loth, loathe
These words are often confused.

If you are **loath** or **loth** to do something, you are very unwilling to do it: *I am loath to change it.*
To **loathe**, with an **e** at the end, is to hate something: *I loathe ironing.*

☆ Remember: I loath**e** that **e** at the end!

## loose, lose
These two words are often confused.

Something **loose** is not firmly held or not close

fitting: *loose trousers.*

To **lose** something is to no longer have it: *Why do you lose your temper?*

To **lose** is also to be beaten: *We win away games and lose home games.*

## luggage

There is a double **g** in luggage.
A similar word with double **g** is:

> **baggage**

## lu<u>sci</u>ous

The "sh" sound in luscious is spelt **sci**.

The ending is **-ous**.

RULE The "uss" sound at the end of an *adjective* is almost always spelt **-ous**.

## lus<u>tre</u>

Lustre ends in **-re**.

*U.S. spelling*
> **luster**

### macabre
The ending of macabre is **-re**.
The "k" sound is spelt with the letter **c**.

### macaroon
The "k" sound in macaroon is spelt with the letter **c**.
There is one **c** and one **r** in macaroon.

### mackerel
The vowel after **mack** in mackerel is **e**.
The ending is **-el**.

### maddening
There is an **e** after the double **d** in maddening that is sometimes missed out in speech.

RULE When an ending which begins with a vowel is added to a word which ends in a single vowel plus a consonant, the consonant is doubled if the *stress* is on the end of the word or if the word has only one part:

   *mad+en+ing > madd+en+ing = maddening*

## magnanimous

The ending of magnanimous is **-ous**.

RULE The "uss" sound at the end of an *adjective* is almost always spelt **-ous**.

☆ Break this word down into smaller parts to help you remember the spelling:

*mag + na + ni + mous*

## mahogany

The ending of mahogany is **-any**.

☆ Break this word down into three smaller words to help you remember the spelling:

*ma + hog + any*

## maintenance

The vowel after the **t** in maintenance is **e**, even though it is connected to the word **maintain**. The ending is **-ance**.

☆ Remember: **ten** main**ten**ance men
☆ Or: The **tenan**t is responsible for building main**tenan**ce.

## malign

There is a silent **g** at the end of malign.

☆ Malign is related to the word **malignant**, where is the **g** is pronounced. If you remember this, it may help you to remember that malign is spelt with a **g**.

## manageable

There is an **e** before the **-able** ending in manageable.

RULE A final silent **E** is usually dropped when an ending which begins with a vowel is added. But this **E** is retained for the endings **-CE** or **-GE** when these letters keep a *soft* sound:

*manage+able* > *manageable*

## manoeuvre

The sequence of vowels in the middle of manoeuvre is **oeu**.
The ending is **-vre**.

## mantelpiece

This word is made up of the words **mantel** plus **piece**:

*mantel+piece = mantelpiece*

There is an **-el** after the **t**.
The **i** comes before the **e**.

RULE **I** before **E** except after **c**, when they make the sound "ee".

## margarine

The "j" sound in margarine is spelt **g**, even though

the letter **g** before **a**, **o**, or **u** usually has a *hard* sound.
The vowel after **g** is **a**, not **e**.

☆ Remember: I like ma**rga**rine and marmalade on toast.
☆ Or break the word down into smaller parts to help you remember the spelling:

  *mar + ga + rine*

## marmalade

The vowel before the **l** is **a**, not **e**.

☆ Remember: I like ma**rma**lade and margarine on toast.
☆ Or break the word down into smaller parts to help you remember the spelling:

  *mar + ma + lade*

## marriage

There is an **i** in marriage before **-age**.
This word has the same ending as:

  **carr**i**age**

This word is made up of the *verb* **marry** plus the *noun suffix* **-age** added at the end.

RULE When an ending is added to a word which ends in a consonant plus **y**, the **y** changes to **i** (unless the ending added already begins with **i**):

  *marry+age > marri+age = marriage*

## martyr
The ending of martyr is **-tyr**.

## marvellous
There are two **l**s in marvellous.

The word is made up of the word **marvel** plus the *adjective suffix* **-ous** added at the end.

RULE When an ending which begins with a vowel is added to a word which ends in a single vowel plus **L**, the **L** is doubled:

   *marvel+ous > marvell+ous = marvellous*

RULE The "uss" sound at the end of an *adjective* is almost always spelt **-ous**.

## massacre
There is a double **s** in massacre.

☆ Or remember: a **mass** of crops in every **acre**

## mathematics
The vowel after **th** is **e**.

☆ Remember: Teach **them** mathematics.

## matinée
This word came into English from French.
There is an *accent* above the first **e** of the **ée** ending.

☆ Break this word down into smaller parts to help

you remember the spelling:
*ma + tin + ée*

## mat<u>t</u>re<u>ss</u>
There is a double **t** and a double **s** in mattress.

☆ Remember: **Matt**'s add**ress** is on the **mattress**.

## mayo<u>nn</u>aise
There is a double **n** in mayonnaise.

☆ Remember: Dip **n**ice **n**ibbles in mayo**nn**aise.

## mea<u>gre</u>
The ending of meagre is **-re**.

*U.S. spelling*
  **meager**

## mean
The different *verb* forms of mean are:
  **means**
  **meaning**
  **meant**

## medallist
There is a double **l** in medallist.

RULE Usually, when the ending **-IST** is added to a word which ends in a consonant plus **L**, the final **L** is not doubled.

However, medallist is an <u>exception</u> to this rule, and the final **l** <u>is</u> doubled:
**medal+ist > medall+ist = medallist**

☆ Remember: The USA was top of the Olympic **medal list**.

## medicine
There is an **i** after **d** in medicine.
The ending is **-ine**.

## medieval *or* mediaeval
There is always an **i** after the **d** in medieval.
It can be spelt with or without an **a** after the **i**. The vowel sound after the **d** can be spelt **ie** or **iae**.
The ending is **-al**.

## Mediterranean
The beginning is **Medi-**, which means "in the middle".
The middle part is **terr**, with one **t** and two **r**s, which means "earth" or "land".
The ending is **-ean**.

RULE The name or names of areas on the map begin with a capital letter.

☆ Break this word down into smaller parts to help you to remember the spelling:
**Medi + terr + an + ean**

## meringue
The vowel after **r** is **i**.
The ending is **-ue**.

## messenger
The vowel after the double **s** is **e**.

☆ Remember that you s**en**d a mess**en**ger.

## meter, metre
These two words sound the same and they are often confused.

A **meter**, ending in **-er**, is a device which measures and records something.
A **metre**, ending in **-re**, is a unit of measurement.

*U.S. spelling for both meanings*
  **meter**

## mileage *or* milage
Mileage can be spelt with or without an **e** in the middle, but the form **mileage** is more common.

## millennium
There are two **l**s and two **n**s in millennium.

## millionaire
There are two **l**s and one **n** in millionaire.

## miner, minor

These two words sound the same and they can be confused.

A **miner**, ending in **-er**, works in a **mine**.
**Minor**, ending in **-or**, means less important or serious than another thing: *a minor incident*.
A **minor** is also someone under eighteen.

These spellings are also often used by mistake for **mynah**, which is the bird that can mimic sounds.

## miniature

There is an **a** after **mini** in miniature.
The ending is **-ture**.

## ministry

There is no **e** in ministry, even though it is related to the *verb* **minister**.

## minuscule

The vowel after **n** in minuscule is **u**.

☆ If you remember the spelling of min**u**te (meaning very small), it may help you to remember that there is a **u** after the **n** in min**u**scule (which also means very small).

## miracle

The vowel after **r** is **a**.

The ending is **-cle**.

A related word is
*adjective* **miraculous**

☆ If you remember the spelling of the word mir**a**culous, where the **a** is more pronounced, it may help you to remember that there is an **a** after the **r** in mir**a**cle.

## miscellaneous
The "ss" sound in miscellaneous is spelt **sc**.
There is a double **l** in the middle.
There is an **e** before **-ous**. The ending is **-eous**.

## mischief
The **i** comes before the **e** in mischief.

RULE **i** before **e** except after **c**, when they make the sound "ee".

A related word is
*adjective* **mischievous**

There is no **i** after the **v** in mischievous.

## misogyny
The beginning of misogyny is **mis-**.
The middle part is **gyn**.

Related words are
*noun* **misogynist**
*adjective* **misogynous**

The word is made up of **miso-** which means "hatred of" plus **-gyny** which means the word relates to women or females.

## misshapen
There is a double **s** in misshapen.

The word is made up of the *adjective* **shapen** plus the *prefix* **mis-** added at the beginning. When the prefix **mis-** is added to a word which begins with **s**, there will be a double **s**:

*mis+shapen = misshapen*

## misspell
There is a double **s** in misspell.

The word is made up of the *verb* **spell** plus the *prefix* **mis-** added at the beginning. When the prefix **mis-** is added to a word which begins with **s**, there will be a double **s**:

*mis+spell = misspell*

## misspent
There is a double **s** in misspent.

The word is made up of **spent**, the *past tense* of the *verb* **spend**, plus the *prefix* **mis-** added at the beginning. When the prefix **mis-** is added to a word which begins with **s**, there will be a double **s**:

*mis+spent = misspent*

## mnemonic

There is a silent **m** at the beginning of mnemonic.
It starts with **mn-**.

☆ Remember: **M**y **N**ephew **E**ric **M**emorizes **O**dd **N**umbers **I**n **C**lass.

## moccasins

There are two **c**s and one **s** in moccasin.

## mongrel

Mongrel begins with **mon-**.

☆ Remember: a **mong**rel from **Mong**olia

## monkey

The ending of monkey is **-ey**.

The *plural* of monkey is:
   **monkeys**

RULE The *plural* of a word which ends in a vowel
plus **y** is made by adding **-s**:
   **monkey+s = monkeys**

## monologue

The beginning of monologue is **mono-**.
The last two letters are **-ue**. The ending is **-gue**.

☆ Remember: His monolog**ue** **u**pset **e**veryone.

**moreover**

Moreover is made up of the words **more** and **over**:

*more + over = moreover*

**mortgage**

There is a silent **t** in mortgage, after the **r**.

☆ Break this word down into two parts to help you remember the spelling:

*mort + gage*

**moustache**

Moustache begins with **mou-**.
The "ash" sound at the end is spelt **-ache**.

☆ Remember: A **mou**stache is above the **mou**th.
☆ Or: Shaving a moust**ache** can give you an **ache**.

*U.S. spelling*
  *mustache*

**museum**

The "mew" sound at the beginning of museum is spelt **mu-**.
The **zz** sound is spelt with a single **s**.

☆ Remember: a **mus**eum of **mus**ic

# mystic

Mystical begins with **mys-**.
The ending is **-ic**.

☆ Break this word down into two parts to help you remember the spelling:

**mys + tic**

# mystify

Mystify begins with **mys-**.

A related word is
*noun **mystification***

☆ Remember: I **mys**tify **mys**elf.

# N

**naive** *or* **naïve**
This is a word which came into English from French.
The vowel sound is spelt **ai**.
There is sometimes an *accent* above the **i**.

A related word is
  noun **naivety** *or* **naiveté**

The spelling **naivety** is the most common.

**nausea**
The first vowel sound is spelt **au**.
The "z" sound is spelt with the letter **s**.
The ending is **-ea**.

Related words include
  verb **nauseate**
  adjective **nauseous**

**necessary**
There is one **c** and a double **s** in necessary.
The ending is **-ary**.

A related word is
  noun **necessity**

☆ Remember: It is ne**cess**ary to have one **c**ollar and two **s**ocks.

## negligent
The vowel after **l** in negligent is **i**, although it is related to the word **neglect**.
The ending is **-ent**.

A related word is
   *noun* **negligence**

## negligible
The vowel after **l** in negligible is **i**, although it is related to the word **neglect**.
The ending is **-ible**.

## nego̲t̲i̲ate
Negotiate starts with **ne-**.
The "sh" sound is spelt **ti**.

A related word is
   *noun* **negotiation**

## ne̲i̲g̲h̲bour
Neighbour begins with the word **neigh**.
The ending is **-our**.

A related word is
   *adjective* **neighbouring**

RULE When the *suffix* **-ING** is added to a word

ending in **-OUR**, the **U** is <u>not</u> dropped from the **-OUR**
ending.

## neither
The **e** comes before the **i** in neither.
The spelling is similar to:
### *either*

## neurotic
The first vowel sound is spelt **eu**. The beginning is
**neu-**.

A related word is
> noun **neurosis**

☆ Remember: The government is n**eu**rotic about
the **E**uropean **U**nion.

## neutral
The first vowel sound is spelt **eu**. The beginning is
**neu-**.

## niche
This is a word which came into English from
French.
The "ee" sound is spelt **i**.
The "sh" sound is spelt **ch**.

## niece
The **i** comes before the **e** in niece.

RULE I before E except after C, when they make the sound "ee".

☆ Remember: My **ni**ece is **ni**ce.

## ninety

Ninety is made up of the word **nine** plus the *suffix* **-ty** added at the end:

   *nine+ty = ninety*

## ninth

There is no **e** in ninth.

## noisily

The vowel after **s** in noisily is **i**.

RULE When an ending is added to a word which ends in a consonant plus **Y**, the **Y** changes to **I** (unless the ending added already begins with **I**):

   *noisy+ly > noisi+ly = noisily*

## noticeable

There is an **e** after the **c** in noticeable.

RULE A final silent **E** is usually dropped when an ending which begins with a vowel is added. But this **E** is retained for the endings **-CE** or **-GE** when these letters keep a *soft* sound:

   *notice+able = noticeable*

☆ Remember that the **e** is noti**ce**able.

### nuance
This is a word which came into English from French.
The first vowel sound is spelt **u**.
The ending is **-ance**.

### nucleus
The ending of nucleus is **-eus**.

### nuisance
The "yoo" sound is spelt **ui**. The beginning is **nui-**.
The ending is **-ance**.

### obscene
The "ss" sound in obscene is spelt **sc**.

A related word is
   noun **obscenity**

### obsess
The first "ss" sound is spelt with a single **s**.
The second "ss" sound is spelt with a double **s**.

Related words are
   noun **obsession**
   adjective **obsessive**

### occasion
There are two **c**s and one **s** in occasion.

Related words are
   adjective **occasional**
   adverb **occasionally**

Occasional is made up of the *noun* **occasion** plus the *adjective suffix* **-al** added at the end, and occasionally is made up of the *adjective* **occasional** with the *adverb suffix* **-ly** added at the end:

_occasion+al = occasional_
_occasional+ly = occasionally_

## o**cc**upy
There are two **c**s in occupy.

Related words are
_noun_ **occupation**
_noun_ **occupancy**
_noun_ **occupant**

## o**cc**ur
There are two **c**s and one **r** in occur.

The different _verb_ forms of occur are:
**occurs**
**occurred**
**occurring**

A related word is
_noun_ **occurrence**

RULE When an ending which begins with a vowel is added to a word which ends in a single vowel plus a consonant, the consonant is doubled if the _stress_ is on the end of the word:
_occur+ed > occurr+ed = occurred_
_occur+ing > occurr+ing = occurring_
_occur+ence > occurr+ence = occurrence_

## odour
Odour ends in **-our**.

*U.S. spelling*
　**odor**

## of, off
These two words are often confused.

**Of** is pronounced "ov" and is used in phrases like:
*a cup of tea*; *a friend of his*.
**Off** is pronounced as it is spelt, and is the opposite of **on**: *They stepped off the plane*; *He went off to work*; *an island off the coast*; *I turned the television off*.

## offence
There are two **f**s in offence.
The ending is **-ence**.

A related word is
　*adjective* **offensive**

The letter after **n** in offensive is **s**, even though it is related to the word **offence**.

## offer
The different *verb* forms of offer are:
　**offers**
　**offering**
　**offered**

RULE When an ending which begins with a vowel
is added to a word which ends in a single vowel
plus a consonant, the consonant is doubled if the
stress is on the end of the word.

The stress in offer is not on the end of the word,
therefore:
*offer+ed = offered*
*offer+ing = offering*


## official
There are two **f**s in official.
The "sh" sound is spelt **ci**.
The ending is **-cial**.

☆ Remember that **offic**ials often work in **offic**es.


## omelette
There is one **m** in omelette.
There is an **e** after the **m**.
There is a double **t** at the end. The ending is **-ette**.

*U.S. spelling*
 **omelet**


## omit
There is only one **m** in omit.

The different *verb* forms of omit are:
 **omits**

*omitting*
*omitted*

RULE When an ending which begins with a vowel is added to a word which ends in a single vowel plus a consonant, the consonant is doubled if the *stress* is on the end of the word:

*omit+ed > omitt+ed = omitted*
*omit+ing > omitt+ing = omitting*

A related word is
*noun* **omission**

There is one **m** and a double **s** in omission.

This word is sometimes confused with **emission**.

An **omission** is something which is **omitted** or left out.
An **emission** is something which is **emitted** or sent out.


## onion
Onion begins with **on-**.
The ending is **-on**.
There is an **i** in the middle.

☆ Break this word down into smaller parts to help you remember the spelling:

*on + i + on*

### opaque
The "k" sound in opaque is spelt **qu**.

### opinion
There is one **p** in opinion.
The ending is **-ion**.

### opponent
There are two **p**s and one **n** in opponent.

A related word is
*verb* **oppose**

### opportunity
There are two **p**s in opportunity.
The vowel after the double **p** is **o**.

### opposite
There are two **p**s in opposite.

Related words are
*verb* **oppose**
*noun* **opposition**

### optimistic
The vowel after **t** in optimistic is **i**.

A related word is
*noun* **optimism**

☆ Remember: **Tim** is op**tim**istic.

## ordinary

There is an **a** after the **n** in ordinary which is sometimes missed out in speech. The ending is **-ary**.

## original

The vowel after **g** is **i**.

Related words are
*noun* **origin**
*adverb* **originally**

☆ Remember: I ori**gin**ally ordered **gin**.

## ornament

The vowel after **n** is **a**.

☆ Remember: What is the **name** of this or**name**nt?

## orthodox

The "aw" sound in orthodox is spelt **or**.
The vowel after **th** is **o**.

☆ Remember that there are three **o**s in **o**rth**o**d**o**x.

## oscillate

The "ss" sound in oscillate is spelt **sc**.
The vowel after **sc** is **i**.
There is a double **l**.

**ostracize** *or* **ostracise**
The ending is **-cize** or **-cise**.

**outrageous**
There is an **e** after the **g** in outrageous.

RULE A final silent **E** is usually dropped when an ending which begins with a vowel is added. But this **E** is retained for the endings **-CE** or **-GE** when these letters keep a *soft* sound:
   *outrage+ous = outrageous*

**overrate**
There are two **r**s in overrate.

The word is made up of the words **over** plus **rate**:
   *over+rate = overrate*

**oxygen**
There is a **y** after **x** in oxygen.
The ending is **-gen**.

# P

**pageant**
The "dj" sound in pageant is spelt **g**.
The ending is **-eant**.

A related word is
  *noun* **pageantry**

**palate, palette, pallet**
These three words are often confused.

The **palate** is the top of the inside of the mouth.
Your **palate** is also your ability to judge the taste
of food and wine: *a coffee to please every palate*.
A **palette** is a plate on which an artist mixes
colours.
A **palette** is also a range of colours: *a natural
palette of earthy colours*.
A **pallet** is a straw-filled bed, a blade used by
potters, or a platform on which goods are stacked.

**palm**
There is a silent **l** before the **m** in palm.

☆ Remember: The p**alm** tree was c**alm** in the

breeze.

# pamphlet
The "f" sound in pamphlet is spelt **ph**.
The ending is **-et**.

# panic
Panic ends in **-ic**.

The different *verb* forms of panic are:
   *panics*
   *panicked*
   *panicking*

RULE When an ending which begins with **E, I,** or **Y**
is added to a word which ends in **c**, a **K** is also
added to the **c** to keep its *hard* sound:
   *panic+ed > panick+ed = panicked*
   *panic+ing > panick+ing = panicking*

# parachute
The vowel after **r** in parachute is **a**. The beginning
is **para-**.
The "sh" sound in parachute is spelt **ch**.
The "oo" sound is spelt **u**, with a final silent **e**.

# paraffin
There is one **r** and two **f**s in paraffin.

☆ Remember: Pa**r**affin **r**eally **f**uels **f**ires.

# parallel

There is one **r** in parallel. The beginning is **para-**.
There are two **l**s in the middle.
There is one **l** at the end. The ending is **-el**.

The different *verb* forms of parallel are
**parallels**
**paralleling**
**paralleled**

RULE Usually, when an ending which begins with a vowel is added to a word which ends in a single vowel plus **L**, the **L** is doubled.

However, **parallel** is an <u>exception</u> to this rule, and the final consonant is <u>not</u> doubled:
**parallel+ed = paralleled**
**parallel+ing = paralleling**

# paralyse

The vowel after **r** in paralyse is **a**. The beginning is **para-**.
The ending is **-yse**.

Related words are
*noun* **paralysis**
*adjective* **paralytic**

# parliament

There is an **i** in parliament, after the **l**.

A related word is

*adjective* ***parliamentary***

☆ Remember: There is a **lia**r in par**lia**ment.
☆ Or: **Liam** is in par**liam**ent.

## par̲ticula̲r

There is an **r** before the **t** in particular. The beginning is **par-**.
The ending is **-ar**.

A related word is
*adverb* ***particularly***

## partner

There is no vowel between the **t** and **n** of partner.

☆ Break this word down into two parts to help you remember the spelling:
***part + ner***

## passed, past

These two spellings are often confused.

**Passed** is the *past tense* of **pass**: *He had passed by the window.*
To go **past** something is to go beyond it: *I drove past without stopping.*
The **past** is the time before the present or describes things which existed before it: *the past few years.*

## passenger
The vowel after **pass** is **e**.

## pastime
There is only one **s** in pastime.

## peace, piece
These two words sound the same and are often confused.

**Peace** is a state of calm and quiet.
A **piece** is a part of something.

☆ Remember: a **pie**ce of **pie**.

## peculiar
The ending of peculiar is **-iar**.

A related word is
  noun **peculiarity**

## pedal, peddle
These two words sound the same and are often confused.

A **pedal** is a lever controlled with the foot.
To **pedal** something is to move its pedals.
To **peddle** something is to sell it illegally.

## pedestrian
Pedestrian begins with **ped-**.

## pend<u>ant</u>
Pendant ends in **-ant**.

## pen<u>e</u>trate
The vowel after **n** in penetrate is **e**.

A related word is
  noun **penetration**

## penicillin
There is one **n** and two **l**s in penicillin.
The vowel after **n** is **i**.
The "ss" sound is spelt **c**.

☆ Remember: You take penic**ill**in when you are
**ill**.

## peninsula, peninsular
These two words are often confused.

**Peninsula** is the *noun*: *The Iberian peninsula
consists of Spain and Portugal.*
**Peninsular** is the *adjective*: *the long peninsular
chin of England; a peninsular city.*

## perc<u>ei</u>ve
The **e** comes before the **i** in perceive.

RULE **i** before **e** except after **c**, when they make
the sound "ee".

A related word is

*adjective* **perceptible**

The ending of perceptible is **-ible**.

## perf<u>o</u>rate
The vowel between **f** and **r** in perforate is **o**.

A related word is
  *noun* **perforation**

## perman<u>ent</u>
The ending of permanent is **-ent**.
The vowel after **m** is **a**.

A related word is
  *noun* **permanence**

## permit
The different *verb* forms of permit are:
  **permits**
  **permitting**
  **permitted**

RULE When an ending which begins with a vowel is added to a word which ends in a single vowel plus a consonant, the consonant is doubled if the *stress* is on the end of the word:
  **permit+ed > permitt+ed = permitted**
  **permit+ing > permitt+ing = permitting**

Related words are
  *noun* **permission**

*adjective* **permissible**

## persist**ent**
Persistent ends in **-ent**.

A related word is
  *noun* **persistence**

## perso**nn**e**l**
There are two **n**s and one **l** in personnel.

This word is sometimes confused with **personal**.

## pers**uade**
The "sw" sound in persuade is spelt **su**.
The ending is **-ade**.

Related words are
  *noun* **persuasion**
  *adjective* **persuasive**

## phenomenon
There is an **m** after the first **o** in phenomenon.
The middle part is **nom**.
The ending is **-non**.

☆ Break this word down into smaller parts to help
you remember the spelling:
  *phe + no + me + non*

## picturesque
The "k" sound in picturesque is spelt **-que**. The ending is **-esque**.

## pie<u>ce</u>, p<u>ea</u>ce
These two words sound the same and are often confused.

A **piece** is a part of something.
**Peace** is a state of calm and quiet.
The **i** comes before the **e** in piece, when it means a part of something.

RULE **I** before **E** except after **c**, when they make the sound "ee".

☆ Remember: a **pie**ce of **pie**.

## pig<u>eon</u>
The "dj" sound in pigeon is spelt **g**.
The ending is **-eon**.

☆ Remember that **pig**eon contains the word **pig**.

## pill<u>ar</u>
There are two **l**s in pillar.
The ending is **-ar**.

☆ Remember: The pi**llar** in the ce**llar** is worth a do**llar**.

## plagiarize *or* plagiarise
The "ay" sound in plagiarize is spelt with an **a** only.

The "j" sound is spelt **g**.
There is an **i** after the **g**. The middle part is spelt **gia**.

A related word is
  noun **plagiarism**

## plague
The ending of plague is **-gue**.

This word can be confused with **plaque**, which looks similar.

## plaque
The ending of plaque is **-que**.

This word can be confused with **plague**, which looks similar.

## plausible
Plausible ends in **-ible**.

A related word is
  noun **plausibility**

## playwright
The ending is **-wright**.

## please

The "ee" sound in please is spelt **ea**.
The ending is **-se**.

☆ Remember: **eas**y to pl**eas**e
☆ Or: Pl**ease** with **ease**

## pleurisy

The "oo" sound in pleurisy is spelt **eu**.
The ending is **-isy**.

## pliers

The "eye" sound in pliers is spelt **i**.
The ending is **-ers**.

☆ Break this word down into two parts to help you remember the spelling:
   *pli + ers*

## pneumonia

Pneumonia begins with a silent **p**.
The "you" sound is spelt **eu**.

☆ Remember: **Pneu**monia **p**robably **n**ever **e**ases **u**p.

## poem

The middle part of poem is **oe**.

Related words are
   noun **poet**
   adjective **poetic**

*noun* **poetry**

☆ Remember: A p**oe**m causes n**o e**nd of pleasure.

## poignant
The middle part of poignant is **gn**.

## pore, pour
These two words sound the same and are often confused.

If you **pore** over something, you study it carefully.
A **pore** is also a small hole in the surface of your skin.
To **pour** something is to let it flow out of a container.
If something **pours** it flows.

## porridge
There is a double **r** in porridge.
The "dj" sound is spelt **dg**. The ending is **-idge**.

☆ Remember: There is porr**idge** in the fr**idge**.

## possess
There is a double **s** in the middle of possess and a double **s** at the end.

Related words are
*noun* **possession**

*adjective* ***possessive***

☆ Remember: You must po**ss**e**ss** two **s**ocks and two **s**hoes.

## po**ss**ible
There is a double **s** in possible.
The ending is **-ible**.

A related word is
  *noun* **possibility**

## pota**to**
Potato ends in **o**.

The *plural* of potato is made by adding **-es**:
  ***potato+es = potatoes***

☆ Remember: My her**oes** eat potat**oes** and tomat**oes**.

## pour, pore
These two words sound the same and are often confused.

To **pour** something is to let it flow out of a container.
If something **pours** it flows.
To **pore** over something is to study it carefully.
A **pore** is also a small hole in the surface of your skin.

## practice, practise

These two spellings are often confused.

**Practice**, ending in **-ce**, is the *noun*: *target practice*; *In practice, his idea won't work*.

**Practise**, ending in **-se**, is the *verb*: *We must practise what we preach*.

Other words where **-ice** is the *noun*, and **-ise** is the *verb* are:

> noun **advice**
> verb **advise**
> noun **device**
> verb **devise**

☆ Remember that **practice** and **practise** have the same endings as **advice** and **advise**: -ce for the *noun*, -se for the *verb*.

☆ Pract**ice** contains the *noun* **ice**, while pract**ise** contains the *verb* **is**.

## precede, proceed

These two words are often confused.

Something which **precedes** another thing happens before it: *Surnames precede personal names in Japan*.

If you **proceed** you start or continue to do something: *young people who proceed to higher education*.

A word related to **precede** is

> noun **precedent**

## prefer

The different *verb* forms of prefer are:

> **prefers**
> **preferring**
> **preferred**

RULE When an ending which begins with a vowel is added to a word which ends in a single vowel plus a consonant, the consonant is doubled if the *stress* is on the end of the word:

> **prefer+ed > preferr+ed = preferred**
> **prefer+ing > preferr+ing = preferring**

Other related words are

> noun **preference**
> adjective **preferential**

If an ending which begins with a vowel is added to a word which ends in a single vowel plus a consonant and the stress moves from the end to the beginning of the word, the final consonant may not be doubled:

> **prefer+ence = preference**

Related words are

> adjective **preferable**
> adverb **preferably**

The above words can be pronounced with the stress on the **pre-** or the **-fer**. The **r** is not doubled:

> **prefer+able = preferable**

*prefer+ably = preferably*

## prejudice
The "dj" sound in prejudice is spelt **j**.

A related word is
  *adjective **prejudiced***

☆ Remember: If you **prejudg**e something, you show **prejud**ice.

## prerogative
There is an **r** after the **p** of prerogative. The beginning is **pre-**.

## prescribe, proscribe
These two words are sometimes confused.

To **prescribe** something is to recommend it: *The doctor will prescribe the right medicine.*
To **proscribe** something is to ban or forbid it: *Athletes were banned from the Olympics for taking proscribed drugs.*

## presence
Presence is spelt with a single **s** at the beginning and a single **c** at the end.
The opposite of presence is also spelt this way:
  **absence**

A related word is
  *adjective **present***

A number of *adjectives* which end in **-ent** are related to *nouns* which end in **-ence**:
**present** > **presence**

# prevalent
The vowel after **v** in prevalent is **a**.
The ending is **-ent**.

# priest
The **i** comes before the **e** in priest.

RULE **I** before **E** except after **C**, when they make the sound "ee".

# primitive
The vowel after **m** in primitive is **i**.

# principal, principle
These words sound the same and they are often confused.

**Principal** means main or most important: *The Festival has two principal themes.*
The **principal** of a school or college is the person in charge.
A **principle** is a general rule, or a belief which you have about the way you should behave: *the basic principles of Marxism; a woman of principle.*
**In principle** means in theory: *The invitation had been accepted in principle.*

☆ Remember: **Le**arn the princip**le**s.

☆ Or: **Pal** up with the princi**pal** and princi**pal** staff.

## privilege
The vowel after **v** in privilege is **i**.
The ending is **-ege**.

A related word is
  *adjective* **privileged**

☆ Remember: It is **vile** to have no pri**vile**ges.

## procedure
There is only one **e** after **c** in procedure.
The ending is **-ure**.

## proceed, precede
These two words are often confused.

If you **proceed** you start or continue to do something: *young people who proceed to higher education*.
Something which **precedes** another thing happens before it: *Surnames precede personal names in Japan*.

## profession
There is one **f** and a double **s** in profession.

A related word is
  *adjective* **professional**

## professor
There is one **f** and a double **s** in professor.
The ending is **-or**.

## profit
The different *verb* forms of profit are:
**profits**
**profiting**
**profited**

A related word is
*adjective* **profitable**

RULE When an ending which begins with a vowel is added to a word which ends in a single vowel plus a consonant, the consonant is doubled if the *stress* is on the end of the word.

The stress in profit is not on the end of the word, therefore:
*profit+ed = profited*
*profit+ing = profiting*
*profit+able = profitable*

## program, programme
These two spellings can be confused.

A **program** is a computer **program**.
You also **program** a computer.
A **programme** is a plan or schedule.
A **programme** is also something on television or radio.

The different *verb* forms of both these spellings are:
   **programs** or **programmes**
   **programmed**
   **programming**

A related word is
   *adjective* **programmable**

RULE When an ending which begins with a vowel is added to a word which ends in a single vowel plus a consonant, the final consonant is doubled if the *stress* is on the end of the word:
   **program+ed** > **programm+ed** = **programmed**
   **program+ing** > **programm+ing** =
   **programming**

*U.S. spelling for all meanings*
   **program**

## promin<u>ent</u>
The ending of prominent is **-ent**.

A related word is
   *noun* **prominence**

## pron<u>u</u>nciation
There is no **o** before the **u** of pronunciation, even though it is connected to the word **pronounce**.

## prope**ll**er

There are two **l**s in propeller.

The word is made up of the *verb* **propel** plus the *noun suffix* **-er** added at the end.

RULE When an ending which begins with a vowel is added to a word which ends in a single vowel plus **L**, the **L** is doubled:

*propel+er > propell+er = propeller*

## prophecy, prophesy

These two spellings are often confused.

**Prophecy**, with a **c**, is the *noun*: *I will never make another prophecy.*
**Prophesy**, with an **s**, is the *verb*: *I can prophesy Scotland will win.*

Other words where the *noun* is spelt with **c** and the *verb* is spelt with **s** are:

noun **advi**c**e**
verb **advi**s**e**
noun **devi**c**e**
verb **devi**s**e**
noun **practi**c**e**
verb **practi**s**e**

☆ Remember that **prophecy** and **prophesy** have the same letter patterns as **advice** and **advise**: **c** for the *noun*, **s** for the *verb*.

## prescribe, proscribe
These two words are sometimes confused.

To **proscribe** something is to ban or forbid it: *Athletes were banned from the Olympics for taking proscribed drugs.*

To **prescribe** something is to recommend it: *The doctor will prescribe the right medicine.*

## prot<u>ei</u>n
The **e** comes before the **i** in protein.

RULE Usually **I** comes before **E** except after **C**, when they make the sound "ee".

However, **protein** is an <u>exception</u> to this rule, with the **e** before the **i**.

## prot<u>o</u>col
The vowel after **t** in protocol is **o**.

☆ Break this word down into smaller parts to help you remember the spelling:

   *pro + to + col*

## prov<u>o</u>cation
The vowel after **v** in provocation is **o**.

☆ Remember that provocation is related to the *verb* **provoke**, and it may help you to remember that it is an **o** after the **v**.

## psalm

Psalm begins with a silent **p**.
There is a silent **l** before the **m**.

## pseudonym

Pseudonym begins with a silent **p**.
The "oo" sound is spelt **eu**.
The vowel after **n** is **y**. The ending is **-nym**.

☆ Remember: Use a pseudo**nym** to stay ano**nym**ous.

## psychedelic

Psychedelic begins with **psych-**, where the **p** is silent.
The vowel which follows is **e**.

## psychiatry
## psychology

Both these words begin with **psych-**, where the **p** is silent.

## pursue

Pursue begins with **pur-**.

A related word is
  *noun* **pursuit**

## pyjamas

Pyjamas begins with **py-**.

*U.S. spelling*
 **pajamas**

## pyramid
Pyramid begins with **py-**.

# Q

## quadruped
The vowel after **r** in quadruped is **u**.

☆ Remember: A quadr**u**ped has fo**u**r legs.

## qualm
There is a silent **l** before the **m** in qualm.

☆ Remember: If you have no qu**alm**s you stay c**alm**.

## quarrel
There are two **r**s in quarrel.
There is one **l** at the end. The ending is **-el**.

The different *verb* forms of quarrel are:
   **quarrels**
   **quarrelled**
   **quarrelling**

RULE When an ending which begins with a vowel is added to a word which ends in a single vowel plus **L**, the **L** is doubled:
   *quarrel+ed > quarrell+ed = quarrelled*
   *quarrel+ing > quarrell+ing = quarrelling*

## query
There is one **e** in query.

The *plural* of query is:
   *queries*

**RULE** The *plural* of a word which ends in a consonant plus **y** is made by changing the **y** to **i** and adding **-es**:
   *query* > *queri+es = queries*

## questionnaire
There are two **n**s in questionnaire.
The ending is **-aire**.

## queue
The vowels after **qu-** are **-eue**.

☆ Break this word down into smaller parts to help you remember the spelling:
   *q + ue + ue*

## quiet, quite
These two words are often confused.

**Quiet** means not noisy.
**Quite** means fairly but not very.

☆ Remember: A qui**et** p**et** can have qu**ite** a b**ite**.

## quiz
There is one **z** in quiz.

The different *verb* forms of quiz are:

**quizzes**
**quizzing**
**quizzed**

The *plural* of quiz is:

**quizzes**

RULE When an ending which begins with a vowel is added to a word which ends in a single vowel plus a consonant, the consonant is doubled if the *stress* is on the end of the word or if the word has only one part:

*quiz+es* > *quizz+es* = *quizzes*
*quiz+ing* > *quizz+ing* = *quizzing*
*quiz+ed* > *quizz+ed* = *quizzed*

# R

### rack, wrack
These two spellings can be confused.

**Rack** *or* **wrack** is an old word for destruction, but the form **rack** is more common: *rack and ruin.*
A **rack** is a framework for storing things.
A **rack** is also an old instrument of torture.
To **rack** is to cause suffering.
To **rack** is also to strain or shake violently: *a nerve-racking moment.*
You **rack** your brains when you try hard to think of something.

### rain, reign, rein
These spellings are often confused.

**Rain** is water falling from the clouds.
To **reign** is to rule a country or be the most noticeable feature of a situation: *Peace reigned while Charlemagne lived.*
**Reins** are straps which control a horse or child.
To **rein** something is to keep it under control: *She reined in her enthusiasm.*

### rancour
Rancour ends in **-our**.

*U.S. spelling*
   **rancor**

### really
There are two **l**s in really.

The word is made up of the *adjective* **real** plus the *adverb suffix* **-ly** added at the end:
   ***real+ly = really***

### rebel
The different *verb* forms of rebel are:
   ***rebels***
   ***rebelling***
   ***rebelled***

A related word is
   *noun* **rebellion**

RULE When an ending which begins with a vowel is added to a word which ends in a single vowel plus **l**, the **l** is doubled:
   ***rebel+ion > rebell+ion = rebellion***
   ***rebel+ed > rebell+ed = rebelled***
   ***rebel+ing > rebell+ing = rebelling***

### recede
The "ss" sound in recede is spelt with a single **c**. The ending is **-ede**.

### receipt

There is a silent **p** before the **t** in receipt.
The beginning is **re-**.
The **e** comes before the **i** at the end.

RULE | I before E except after **c**, when they make the sound "ee".

### receive

Receive begins with **re-**.
The **e** comes before the **i** at the end.

RULE | I before E except after **c**, when they make the sound "ee".

### recognize or recognise

There is a **g** after the **o** in recognize.

### recommend

There is one **c** and two **m**s in recommend.

The word is made up of the *verb* **commend** plus the *prefix* **re-**, which indicates repetition, added at the beginning.

A related word is
    noun **recommendation**

### reconnaissance

There is a double **n** and a double **s** in reconnaissance.
The ending is **-ance**.

## recur

There is one **r** at the end of recur.

The different *verb* forms of recur are:
**recurs**
**recurring**
**recurred**

Other related words are
*noun* **recurrence**
*adjective* **recurrent**

RULE When an ending which begins with a vowel is added to a word which ends in a single vowel plus a consonant, the consonant is doubled if the *stress* is on the end of the word:
**recur+ing > recurr+ing = recurring**
**recur+ed > recurr+ed = recurred**
**recur+ence > recurr+ence = recurrence**
**recur+ent > recurr+ent = recurrent**

## redundant

Redundant ends in **-ant**.

A related word is
*noun* **redundancy**

## refer

The different *verb* forms of refer are:
**refers**
**referring**
**referred**

A related word is
> noun **referral**

RULE When an ending which begins with a vowel
is added to a word which ends in a single vowel
plus a consonant, the consonant is doubled if the
*stress* is on the end of the word:
> **refer+ing > referr+ing = referring**
> **refer+ed > referr+ed = referred**
> **refer+al > referr+al = referral**

Other related words are
> noun **referee**
> noun **reference**

If an ending which begins with a vowel is added
to a word which ends in a single vowel plus a
consonant and the stress changes so that it is no
longer on the end of the word, the final consonant
may not be doubled:
> **refer+ee = referee**
> **refer+ence = reference**

### refrigerator
There is no **d** in refrigerator, although the
shortened form is **fridge**. The "dj" sound is made
by **g** only.

### regret
The different *verb* forms of regret are:
> **regrets**

> *regretting*
> *regretted*

A related word is
> *adjective* **regrettable**

RULE When an ending which begins with a vowel is added to a word which ends in a single vowel plus a consonant, the consonant is doubled if the *stress* is on the end of the word:

> *regret+ing > regrett+ing = regretting*
> *regret+ed > regrett+ed = regretted*
> *regret+able > regrett+able = regrettable*

## reh<u>ea</u>rse

The vowel sound in rehearse is spelt **ea**.
The ending is **-rse**.

A related word is
> *noun* **rehearsal**

☆ Remember: I **hear** there is a re**hear**sal.

## reign, rein, rain

These spellings are often confused.

To **reign** is to rule a country or be the most noticeable feature of a situation: *Peace reigned while Charlemagne lived.*
**Reins** are straps which control a horse or child.
To **rein** something is to keep it under control: *She reined in her enthusiasm.*

**Rain** is water falling from the clouds.

## relevant
The vowel after **l** is **e**.
The ending is **-ant**.

A related word is
  noun **relevance**

☆ Break this word down into smaller parts to help
you remember the spelling:
  *re + le + vant*

## relieve
The beginning of relieve is **re-**.
For the "ee" sound after the **l**, the **i** comes before
the **e**.

Rule  I before E except after C, when they make
the sound "ee".

A related word is
  noun **relief**

## religion
Religion begins with **re-**.

A related word is
  adjective **religious**

## reminisce
The "ss" sound in reminisce is spelt **sc**. The ending

is **-isce**.

A related word is
*adjective* **reminiscent**

## remi**tt**ance
There is one **m** and two **t**s in remittance.
The ending is **-ance**.

RULE When an ending which begins with a vowel
is added to a word which ends in a single vowel
plus a consonant, the final consonant is doubled if
the *stress* is on the end of the word:

*remit+ance > remitt+ance = remittance*

## remu**n**eration
The **m** comes before the **n** in remuneration.

☆ Remember: **Re**ward **mu**st **ne**ed **remune**ration.
☆ Or break this word down into smaller parts to
help you remember the spelling:

*re + mu + ne + ra + tion*

## rendezvous
This word came into English from French.

The beginning is **ren-**.
There is a **z** before the **v**.
The ending is spelt **-ous**, with a silent **s**.

☆ Break this word down into smaller parts to help
you remember the spelling:

*ren + dez + vous*

## renunciation
There is no **o** before the **u** of renunciation, even though it is connected to the word **renounce**.

## repentant
Repentant ends in **-ant**.

## repertoire
There is an **r** before the **t** in repertoire.
There is an **e** at the end. The ending is **-oire**.

☆ Remember: Every **per**son has their re**per**toire.

## repetition
The vowel after **p** in repetition is **e**.

A related word is
   *adjective* **repetitive**

The vowel after the first **t** in repetitive is **i**.

☆ Remember that repetition is connected to the *adjective* rep**e**titive where the **e** is more pronounced, and it may help you to remember that the vowel after **p** in rep**e**tition is **e**.
☆ Remember that repetitive is connected to the *noun* repet**i**tion where the **i** is more pronounced, and it may help you to remember that the vowel after the first **t** in repet**i**tive is **i**.

## reprieve

The **i** comes before the **e** in reprieve.

RULE I before E except after **c**, when they make the sound "ee".

## resemble

There is one **s** in resemble.

A related word is
*noun* **resemblance**

RULE A final silent **E** is dropped when an ending which begins with a vowel is added:
*resemble+ance > resembl+ance = resemblance*

☆ Remember that something which re**s**embles something else has the **s**emblance of it.

## reservoir

There is an **r** before the **v** in reservoir.
The ending is **-oir**.

☆ Remember that a **reserv**oir is where water is kept in **reserv**e.

## resign

There is a silent **g** before the **n** in resign.

A related word is
*noun* **resignation**

☆ Remember that resign is connected to the word resignation where the **g** is pronounced, and it may help you to remember the **g** in resi**g**n.

## resis**t**ance
Resistance has the ending **-ance**.

A related word is
  *adjective* **resistant**

## respon**sible**
Responsible begins with **re-**.
The ending is **-ible**.

A related word is
  *noun* **responsibility**

## rest**au**rant
This word came into English from French.

The vowel sound after **rest-** is spelt **au**.
The ending is **-ant**.

☆ Break this word down into smaller parts to help you remember the spelling:
  *res + tau + rant*

## resu**rr**ection
Resurrection has a double **r** in the middle.

☆ Remember: A resu**rr**ection is a **r**epeat **r**ise.

## retrieve
The **i** comes before the **e** in retrieve.

RULE **I** before **E** except after **C**, when they make the sound "ee".

A related word is
*noun* **retrieval**

RULE A final silent **E** is dropped when an ending which begins with a vowel is added:
**retrieve+al > retriev+al = retrieval**

## reversible
Reversible ends in **-ible**.

## rheumatism
Rheumatism begins with **rh-**.
The "oo" sound is spelt **eu**.

A related word is
*adjective* **rheumatic**

☆ Remember: A **rh**eumatic **rh**inoceros eats **rh**ubarb.

## rhinoceros
Rhinoceros begins with **rh-**.
The "ss" sound in the middle is spelt with a single **c**.
The ending is **-os**.

☆ Remember: A **rh**eumatic **rh**inoceros eats

**rh**ubarb.

## rhubarb
Rhubarb begins with **rh-**.

☆ Remember: A **rh**eumatic **rh**inoceros eats **rh**ubarb.

## rhyme
Rhyme begins with **rh-**.
The sound "eye" is spelt **y**.

## rhythm
Rhythm begins with **rh-**.
The "i" sound is spelt **y**.
There is no vowel at the end. It is simply spelt **-thm**.

☆ Remember: **R**oger **H**ates **Y**our **T**rendy **H**eavy **M**etal.

## ridiculous
Ridiculous begins with **ri-**.

A related word is
  *noun* **ridicule**

## righteous
There is an **e** after **right** in righteous.
This is followed by **-ous**.

RULE The "uss" sound at the end of an *adjective* is

almost always spelt **-OUS**.

## rigor, rigour

These two spellings can be confused.

**Rigor mortis** is the stiffening of a dead body.
**Rigours** are difficult or demanding things about an activity: *the rigours of the football season*.
**Rigour** is strictness or thoroughness: *intellectual rigour*.

A related word is
   *adjective* **rigorous**

RULE When the *adjective ending* **-OUS** is added to a word ending in **-OUR**, the **U** of the **-OUR** is dropped:

   ***rigour+ous* > *rigor+ous* = *rigorous***

RULE The "uss" sound at the end of an *adjective* is almost always spelt **-OUS**.

*U.S. spelling for all meanings*
   *rigor*

## ring, wring

These two words sound the same and can be confused.

A **ring** is the sound made by a bell.
A **ring** is also a circle or enclosure.
To **wring** something is to twist it.

☆ Remember: You **w**ring out something **w**et.

**ro_gue_**
The ending of rogue is **-gue**.

**rum_our_**
Rumour ends in **-our**.

*U.S. spelling*
  ***rumor***

# S

## sacrifice
There is no letter between the **c** and **r** of sacrifice.
The vowel after **r** is **i**.

## sacrilege
The vowel after **r** in sacrilege is **i**.
The ending is **-ege**.

A related word is
   *adjective* **sacrilegious**

## sandwich
There is a **d** after the **n** in sandwich.

The *plural* of sandwich is:
   **sandwiches**

RULE The *plural* of a word which ends in **s**, **x**, **z**, **sh**, or **ch** is made by adding **-es**.

☆ Remember: There is **sand** in these **sand**wiches.
☆ Or break this word down into smaller parts to help you remember the spelling:
   **sand + wich**

# sapphire
There is a double **p** in sapphire.

☆ Remember: You would be ha**pp**y to get a sa**pp**hire.

# satellite
There is one **t** and two **l**s in satellite.

☆ Remember: **Tell** me about the sa**tell**ite.
☆ Or break this word down into smaller parts to help you remember the spelling:
   *sa + tell + ite*

# sausage
The "aw" sound in sausage is spelt **au**.
The ending is **-age**.

# scarf
The *plural* of scarf is:
   **scarves** or **scarfs**

The form **scarves** is much more common.

# sceptic
Sceptic, pronounced skep-tik, begins with **sc-**.

A related word is
   *adjective* **sceptical**

   *U.S. spellings*
   **skeptic**
   **skeptical**

## schedule
Schedule begins with **sch-**.

☆ Remember: a **sch**ool **sch**edule

## schizophrenia
Schizophrenia begins with **sch-**.
There is a **z** after the **i**.
The **z** is followed by **o**.
The "f" sound is spelt **ph**.

A related word is
   *noun, adjective* **schizophrenic**

## science
Science begins with **sc-**.
The ending is **-ence**.

A related word is
   *noun* **scientist**

## scissors
Scissors begins with **sc-**.
There is a double **s** in the middle.
The ending is **-ors**.

## scythe
Scythe begins with **sc-**.
There is an **e** at the end.

☆ Break this word down into two parts to help you remember the spelling:
   *scy + the*

## secondary
There is an **a** after the **d** in second<u>a</u>ry which is sometimes missed out in speech. The ending is **-ary**.

## secretary
The vowel after **cr** in secret<u>a</u>ry is **e**.
There is an **a** after the **t** which is sometimes missed out in speech. The ending is **-ary**.

A related word is
   *adjective* **secretarial**

☆ Remember the spelling of the *adjective* secret**a**rial, where the **a** is more pronounced, and it may help you to remember that there is an **a** in the ending of secret**a**ry.
☆ And remember: a **secret secret**ary.

## seize
The **e** comes before the **i** in s<u>ei</u>ze.

RULE Usually **I** comes before **E** except after **C**, when they make the sound "ee".

However, **seize** is an <u>exception</u> to this rule, with the **e** before the **i**.

A related word is
*noun* **seizure**

## separate

The vowel after **p** in separate is **a**. The middle section is **par**.

Related words are
*noun* **separation**
*adjective* **separable**

☆ Remember: There's **a rat** in sep**arat**e.
☆ Or: Two boys started fighting and their **pa** had to se**pa**rate them.

## septic

Septic begins with **se-**.

This word can be confused with **sceptic**, but remember that sceptic is pronounced skep-tik.

## sergeant

The vowel after **s** is **e**. Sergeant begins with **ser-**. The "dj" sound in the middle is spelt with a **g** only. The vowel sound after **g** is spelt **ea**.

## serial, cereal

These two words are sometimes confused.

A **serial** is something published or broadcast in a number of parts.

**Serial** also describes other things that happen in a **series**.
**Cereal** is food made from grain.

**Serial** begins with **se-**.
The ending is **-ial**.

## series
Series begins with **se-**.
The ending is **-ies**.

## serious
Serious begins with **se-**.
The ending is **-ious**.

## se<u>tt</u>ee
There is a double **t** in settee.
It ends in double **e**.

☆ Remember: **Sett**le down on the **sett**ee.

## sev<u>e</u>ral
There is an **e** after the **v** in several.

☆ Remember: If you have **seve**n items then you have **seve**ral.

## sheikh *or* sheik
Sheik *or* sheikh, meaning an Arab chief, can be spelt with **kh** or **k** at the end.
The "ay" sound is spelt **ei**.

## shepherd

There is an **h** after the **p** in shepherd.

☆ Remember that a shep**herd** is someone who **herd**s sheep.

## shield

The **i** comes before the **e** in shield.

RULE I before E except after C, when they make the sound "ee".

## shining

There is no **e** in shining.

RULE A final silent E is dropped when an ending which begins with a vowel is added:

*shine+ing > shin+ing = shining*

## shoot

This spelling can be confused with **chute**, a steep slope for sliding things down.

## shoulder

The "oh" sound in shoulder is spelt **ou**.

This word is sometimes confused with **soldier**.

## siege

The **i** comes before the **e** in siege.

RULE I before E except after C, when they make

the sound "ee".

## s**ie**ve
Sieve, pronounced "siv", contains the vowels **ie**.
There is an **e** after the **v** at the end.

☆ Remember: A **sieve** is for **si**fting **eve**rything.

## sil**h**ouette
Silhouette has a silent **h** after the **l**.
The "oo" sound is spelt **ou**.

☆ Break this word down into smaller parts to help
you remember the spelling:
   *sil + hou + ette*

## similar
There is one **m** and one **l** in similar.
The vowel after **m** is **i**.
The ending is **-ar**.

A related word is
   *noun* **similarity**

## simultan**e**ous
There is an **e** before the **-ous** ending in
simultaneous.

RULE The "uss" sound at the end of an *adjective* is
almost always spelt **-ous**.

☆ Break this word down into smaller parts to help

you remember the spelling:
 *si + mul + tan + e + ous*

## sinc<u>e</u>rely

There is an **e** after the **r** in sincerely.
There is <u>no</u> **e** after the **l**.

The word is made up of the *adjective* **sincere** with
the *adverb suffix* **-ly** added at the end.

RULE  A final silent **E** is dropped when an ending
which begins with a vowel is added, but may not
be dropped when an ending which begins with a
consonant is added:
 *sincere+ly = sincerely*

## skel<u>e</u>ton

There is one **l** in skeleton.
The vowel after **l** is **e**.

☆  Remember: Should you **let on** about the
ske**leton**s in your cupboard?
☆  Or break this word down into smaller parts to
help you remember the spelling:
 *ske + le + ton*

## ski<u>lf</u>ul

There is only one **l** after **i** in skilful.
It ends in a single **l**.

RULE  The *suffix* **-FUL** is always spelt with one **L**.

## slaughter

The "aw" sound in slaughter is spelt **au**.
The **au** is followed by **gh**. The middle part is **augh**.

☆ Remember: You won't hear **laughter** at s**laughter**.

## sleigh

The "ay" sound in sleigh, meaning a sledge, is spelt **ei**.
There is a silent **gh** at the end.

This is a different spelling from the word **slay**, meaning to kill.

☆ Remember: **Eigh**t sl**eigh**s will w**eigh** a lot.

## solemn

There is a silent **n** at the end of solemn.

A related word is
    *noun* **solemnity**

☆ Remember that solemn is related to the word solemnity, where the **n** is clearly pronounced, and it may help you to remember that there is an **n** at the end.
☆ Or remember: I am solem**n**ly condem**n**ed to build a colum**n** in the autum**n**.

**solicitor**
There is one **l** in solicitor.
The ending is **-or**.

**sombre**
Sombre ends in **-re**.

*U.S. spelling*
**somber**

**somersault**
The "uh" sound in somersault is spelt **o**. The beginning is **som-**.
The "aw" sound is spelt **au**.

☆ Remember: **Some** people turn **some**rsaults.

**soothe**
There is an **e** at the end of soothe.

The different *verb* forms of soothe are:
**soothes**
**soothing**
**soothed**

**souvenir**
This is a word which came into English from French.

The "oo" sound is spelt **ou**.
The ending is **-ir**.

# sov<u>e</u>re<u>ign</u>

There is an **e** after the **v** in sovereign.

There is a silent **g** at the end. The ending is **-eign**.

☆ Remember: The sove**reign reign**s.


# spag<u>hetti</u>

This is an Italian word.

There is an **h** after the **g**.

There are two **t**s at the end, before the final **i**.


# special

The "sh" sound in special is spelt **ci**.

The ending is **-al**. The last part is spelt **-cial**.

☆ Remember: A spe**cial** offi**cial** commer**cial** is cru**cial**.


# spontan<u>e</u>ous

There is an **e** before the **-ous** ending in spontaneous.

RULE The "uss" sound at the end of an *adjective* is almost always spelt **-ous**.

☆ Break this word down into smaller parts to help you remember the spelling:

*spon + tan + e + ous*

## squalor
There is one **l** in squalor.
The ending is **-or**.

## stationary, stationery
These two words are very often confused.

**Stationary**, with an **a**, means not moving.
**Stationery**, with an **e**, is paper, pens, and other writing equipment.

☆ Remember: **E**nvelopes are station**e**ry.
☆ Or: Station**e**ry is l**e**tters, but station**a**ry is st**a**nding still.

## steadfast
There is an **a** after the **e** in steadfast.

☆ Remember: If you are **stead**fast you stay **stead**y.

## stealth
The vowel sound in stealth is spelt **ea**.

A related word is
  *adjective* **stealthy**

## stereo
There is an **e** after the **r** in stereo. The ending is **-eo**.

☆ Remember: ste**reo** **re**cords

## stomach

The "uh" sound in stomach is spelt **o**.
There is one **m**.
The "k" sound at the end is spelt **ch**. The ending is
**-ach**.

☆ Remember: A sto**mach** is like a **mach**ine.

## strength

There is a **g** after the **n** in strength.
Another word like this is:
> *length*

☆ Remember that stren**g**th is connected to the
*adjective* stron**g**, and it may help you to
remember the **g**.

## subtle

There is a silent **b** before the **t** in subtle.

Related words are
> noun **subtlety**
> adverb **subtly**

RULE When the *adverb suffix* **-LY** is added to an
*adjective* which ends in a consonant followed by
**-LE**, the **-LE** is usually dropped:
> **subtle+ly** > **subt+ly** = **subtly**

☆ Remember: A **sub**marine moves **sub**tly.

## succeed

There is a double **c** in succeed.
The "ee" sound is spelt **ee**. The ending is **-eed**.

A related word is
   *adjective* **successive**

There is a double **c** and a double **s** in successive.

## success

There is a double **c** and a double **s** in success.

A related word is
   *adjective* **successful**

RULE The *suffix* **-FUL** is always spelt with one **L**.

## succinct

There is a double **c** in the middle of succinct.

☆ Remember: Your speech must be **succ**inct to
be a **succ**ess.

## suddenness

There are two **n**s in suddenness.

The word is made up of the *adjective* **sudden** plus
the *noun suffix* **-ness** added at the end. When the
suffix **-ness** is added to a word which ends with
**n**, there will be two **n**s:
   *sudden+ness = suddenness*

# suede
The "sw" sound in suede is spelt **su-**.
The rest is spelt **-ede**.

☆ Remember: bl**ue** s**ue**de shoes
☆ Or: **Sue de**manded **suede** shoes.

# sufficient
There is a double **f** in sufficient.
The "sh" sound is spelt **ci**.
The ending is **-ent**.

A related word is
  noun **sufficiency**

# suffocate
There is a double **f** in suffocate.
The **ff** is followed by **o**.

A related word is
  noun **suffocation**

# superintendent
Superintendent ends in **-ent**.

☆ Remember: There is a **dent** in the
superinten**dent**.

# supersede
The "ss" sounds in supersede are both spelt with
a single **s**.
The ending is **-sede**.

## supplement
There is a double **p** in supplement.
The vowel between **l** and **m** is **e**.

A related word is
  *adjective* **supplementary**

☆ Remember that **supple**ment contains the word **supple**.

## suppose
There are two **p**s in suppose.

Related words are
  *adjective* **supposed**
  *noun* **supposition**

## suppress
There is a double **p** and a double **s** in suppress.

A related word is
  *noun* **suppression**

## surgeon
The "dj" sound in surgeon is spelt **g**.
There is an **e** after the **g**. The ending is **-eon**.

☆ Remember: Sur**ge**ons **g**ive **e**ffective **o**perations.

## surplus
Surplus begins with **sur-**.

There is a single **s** at the end. The ending is **-plus**.

☆ Break this word down into smaller parts to help you remember the spelling:

*sur + plus*

## surprise
There is an **r** before the **p** in surprise which is sometimes missed out in speech.

## surveillance
The "ay" sound in surveillance is spelt **ei**.
This is followed by a double **l**.
The ending is **-ance**.

☆ Remember: Bra**ve** **ill** people need sur**veill**ance.

## susceptible
The second "ss" sound in susceptible is spelt **sc**.
The ending is **-ible**.

## suspicious
The "sh" sound in suspicious is spelt **ci**.

RULE The "uss" sound at the end of an *adjective* is almost always spelt **-ous**.

A related word is
*noun* **suspicion**

## sustenance

The vowel after the **t** in sustenance is **e**, even
though it is connected to the word **sustain**.
The ending is **-ance**.

☆ Remember: sus**ten**ance for **ten** people

## symbol

Symbol begins with **sy-**.
The ending is **-ol**.

This word can be confused with **cymbal**, the
percussion instrument.

A related word is
  adjective **symbolic**

☆ Remember the spelling of the adjective
symb**o**lic, where the **o** is more pronounced, and it
may help you to remember that there is an **o** in
symb**o**l.

## symmetry

Symmetry begins with **sy-**.
It has a double **m**.
The vowel after **mm** is **e**.
The ending is **-try**.

A related word is
  adjective **symmetrical**

☆ Remember: **Try** to get symme**try**.
☆ Or remember that apart from the **m**s, the word

**symmetry** is not symmetrical!

## synagogue
Synagogue begins with **sy-**.
It ends in **-gue**.

☆ Remember wh**y** there is no sin in the **syn**agogue!

## synonym
Synonym begins with **sy-**.
This is followed by **no-**.
The ending is **-nym**.

☆ Break this word down into smaller parts to help you remember the spelling:
   *sy + no + nym*

## synthetic
Synthetic begins with **sy-**.

Related words are
   noun **synthesis**
   verb **synthesize** or **synthesise**

## syringe
Syringe begins with **sy-**.
The ending is **-inge**.

# T

### taciturn
The "ss" sound in taciturn is spelt **c**.
The ending is **-urn**.

### taffeta
There are two **f**s in taffeta.
The vowel after **ff** is **e**.

### tangible
The "j" sound in tangible is spelt **g**.
The ending is **-ible**.

### tattoo
There is a double **t** and a double **o** in **tattoo**.

The different *verb* forms of tattoo are:
*tattoos*
*tattooing*
*tattooed*

### temperamental
There is an **e** in temperamental which is often missed out in speech.

A related word is

*noun* **temperament**

☆ Remember that temperamental is related to the word **temper**, and it may help you to remember that there is an **e** between the **p** and **r** in temp**e**ramental.

## temperature
There is an **e** in temperature which is often missed out in speech.
The ending is **-ture**.

☆ Remember that temperature is related to the words **temper** and **temperate**, and it may help you to remember that there is an **e** between the **p** and **r** in temp**e**rature.

## temporary
There is an **o** between the **p** and **r** of temporary which is sometimes missed out in speech.

☆ Remember that **tempo**rary includes the word **tempo**.

## terrible
There is a double **r** in terrible.
There is a similar double **r** in:
  *ho**rr**ible*

The ending is **-ible**.

## terror

There is a double **r** in terror.
There is a similar double **r** in:

**ho_rr_or**

A related word is
*verb* **terrify**
*adjective* **terrified**

RULE When an ending is added to a word which ends in a consonant plus **y**, the **y** changes to **i** (unless the ending added already begins with **i**):

**terrify+ed > terrifi+ed = terrified**

## terrorist

There is a double **r** followed by a single **r** in terrorist.
There is an **o** between the **rr** and the **r**.

The word is made up of the *noun* **terror** plus the *suffix* **-ist** added at the end:

**terror+ist = terrorist**

Related words are
*noun* **terrorism**
*verb* **terrorize** or **terrorise**

## theatre

The vowel sound after **th** in theatre is spelt **ea**.
The ending is **-re**.

*U.S. spelling*

*theater*

## their, there, they're
These spellings are often confused.

**Their** is the spelling used to refer to something belonging or relating to people or things which have already been mentioned: *people who bite their nails*; *It was their fault.*

**There** is the spelling for the word which says that something does or does not exist, draws attention to something, or says that something is at, in, or going to that place: *There is no life on Jupiter*; *There's Kathleen*; *They wanted me there.*

**They're**, with an *apostrophe*, is a shortened form of **they are**: *They're a good team.*

RULE In shortened forms of words or combinations of words with an *apostrophe*, the apostrophe appears in the place where a letter or letters have been missed out:

*they+are > they+re = they're*

## thief
The **i** comes before the **e** in **thief**.

RULE I before E except after C, when they make the sound "ee".

## thinness
There are two **n**s in thinness.

The word is made up of the *adjective* **thin** plus the *suffix* **-ness** added at the end. When the suffix **-ness** is added to a word which ends with **n**, there will be two **ns**:

*thin+ness = thinness*

## thorough

The vowel after the **th** in thorough is spelt with a single **o**.
The ending is **-ough**.

☆ Remember: You don't have to be **rough** to be tho**rough**.

## threshold

There is only one **h** in threshold.

## through, threw

These two words sound the same and they can be confused.

**Through** means going from one side to the other: *They walked through the dense undergrowth.*
**Threw** is the *past tense* of **throw**: *Youths threw stones at passing cars.*

## tide, tied

These two words sound the same and they can be confused.

The **tide** is change in sea level.
**Tied** is the *past tense* of **tie**.

## tire, tyre
These two words sound the same and are sometimes confused.

The rubber ring round the wheel of a vehicle is a **tyre**, spelt with a **y**.

*U.S. spelling (for both meanings)*
    *tire*

## ti<u>ss</u>ue
There is a double **s** in the middle of tissue.
The ending is **-ue**.

☆ Remember: T**issue** is an **issue**.

## toffee
There is a double **f** in the middle of toffee.
There is a double **e** at the end.

☆ Remember: Co**ffee** and to**ffee** have double **f** and double **e**.

## tomat<u>o</u>
**Tomato** ends in **o**.

The *plural* of **tomato** is made by adding **-es**:
    *tomato+es = tomatoes*

☆ Remember: My her**oes** eat tomat**oes** and potat**oes**.

## tomorrow

There is one **m** and two **r**s in tomorrow.

## tongue

The vowel sound in tongue is spelt **o**.
The last two letters are **-ue**. The ending is **-gue**.

☆ Break this word down into two parts to help you remember the spelling:

*ton + gue*

## tragedy

The "dj" sound in tragedy is spelt with a **g** only.

☆ Remember: I **raged** at the t**raged**y.

## tranquil

There is only one **l** at the end of tranquil.

Related words are
*noun* **tranquillity**
*noun* **tranquillizer** *or* **tranquilliser**

RULE When an ending which begins with a vowel is added to a word which ends in a single vowel plus **L**, the **L** is doubled:

*tranquil+ity > tranquill+ity = tranquillity*
*tranquil+izer > tranquill+izer = tranquillizer*

## transcend
The "ss" sound in transcend is spelt **sc**.
Similar words with **sc** are:
  **a<u>sc</u>end**
  **de<u>sc</u>end**

## transfer
The different *verb* forms of transfer are:
  **transfers**
  **transferring**
  **transferred**

RULE When an ending which begins with a vowel is added to a word which ends in a single vowel plus a consonant, the consonant is doubled if the *stress* is on the end of the word. The consonant is also doubled if the stress moves from the beginning to the end of the word when the ending is added:
  **transfer+ing > transferr+ing = transferring**
  **transfer+ed > transferr+ed = transferred**

Another related word is
  *adjective* **transferable**

**Transferable** is an <u>exception</u> to the above rule, and is spelt with one **r** even though the stress moves to the **-fer** part.

## transmit
The different *verb* forms of transmit are:

**transmits**
**transmitting**
**transmitted**

RULE When an ending which begins with a vowel is added to a word which ends in a single vowel plus a consonant, the consonant is doubled if the *stress* is on the end of the word:

**transmit+ed > transmitt+ed = transmitted**
**transmit+ing > transmitt+ing = transmitting**

A related word is
    *noun* **transmission**

## travel
The different verb forms of travel are:
    **travels**
    **travelled**
    **travelling**

RULE When an ending which begins with a vowel is added to a word which ends in a single vowel plus **L**, the **L** is doubled:

**travel+ed > travell+ed = travelled**
**travel+ing > travell+ing = travelling**

## treacherous
The first vowel sound in treacherous is spelt **ea**. There is no **t** after **ea**, just **ch**.

A related word is
    *noun* **treachery**

RULE The "uss" sound at the end of an *adjective* is almost always spelt **-ous**.

☆ Remember: A **trea**cherous person is likely to commit **trea**son.

## tremor
There is only one **m** in tremor.
There is no **u** before the **r**.

## truly
There is no **e** in truly.

## tuberculosis
The vowel after **c** in tuberculosis is **u**.

☆ Break this word down into smaller parts to help you remember the spelling:
   *tu + ber + cu + lo + sis*

## turnstile
There is no **y** in turnstile. The vowel after **st** is **i**.

☆ Remember: You don't need **style** to operate a **turnstile**.

## twelfth
There is an **f** in twelfth, before the **th**.

The **-ve** of **twelve** changes to **f** before the **-th** is added:
   *twelve+th > twelf+th = twelfth*

A similar word is:
  *five+th* > *fif+th* = **fifth**

## typical
There is a **y** between the **t** and the **p** in typical. The ending is **-al**.

A related word is
  adverb **typically**

☆ Remember that typical is related to the word **type**, and it may help you to remember that there is a **y** between the **t** and **p** in typical.

## tyranny
There is a **y** between the **t** and the **r** in tyranny. There is a double **n**.

A related word is
  noun **tyrant**

There is only one **n** in tyrant.

☆ Remember: The mayor of the ci**ty ran N**ew **Y**ork with **tyranny**, while the captain of the Boun**ty ran t**he ship like a **tyrant**.

## tyre, tire
These two words sound the same and are sometimes confused.

The rubber ring round the wheel of a vehicle is a **tyre**, spelt with a **y**.

*U.S. spelling (for both meanings)*
  **tire**

# U

## unconscious

The "sh" sound in unconscious is spelt **sci**.

**RULE** The "uss" sound at the end of an *adjective* is almost always spelt **-ous**.

## underrate

There is a double **r** in underrate. It is made up of the word **under** plus the word **rate**:

*under+rate = underrate*

## unduly

There is no **e** after the **u** in unduly.

## unforgettable

There are two **t**s in unforgettable.

**RULE** When an ending which begins with a vowel is added to a word which ends in a single vowel plus a consonant, the consonant is doubled if the *stress* is on the end of the word:

*unforget+able > unforgett+able = unforgettable*

## unfortunate

There is no **e** after the **n** in unfortunate.

RULE A final silent **E** is dropped when an ending which begins with a vowel is added:
*un+fortune+ate > un+fortun+ate = unfortunate*

A related word is
*adverb **unfortunately***

**Unfortunately** is made up of the *adjective* **unfortunate** plus the *adverb suffix* **-ly** added at the end:
*unfortunate+ly = unfortunately*

☆ Remember: Unfor**tunate**ly the **tuna** she **ate** was bad.

## unnatural

This word is made up of the *adjective* **natural** plus the *prefix* **un-** added at the beginning. When the prefix **un-** is added to a word beginning with **n**, there will be two **n**s:
*un+natural = unnatural*

## unnecessary

This word is made up of the *adjective* **necessary** plus the *prefix* **un-** added at the beginning. When the prefix **un-** is added to a word beginning with **n**, there will be two **n**s:
*un+necessary = unnecessary*

There is one **c** and a double **s** in unnecessary.
The ending is **-ary**.

☆ Remember: It is ne**cess**ary to have one **c**ollar and two **s**ocks.

## until
There is only one **l** at the end of until.

## unwieldy
The **i** comes before the **e** in unwieldy.

Ruᴇ **I** before **E** except after **c**, when they make the sound "ee".

## upheaval
There is no **e** after the **v** in upheaval.

Ruᴇ A final silent **E** is dropped when an ending which begins with a vowel is added:
   *upheave+al* > *upheav+al* = *upheaval*

## used to
Used to is usually spelt with a **d**.

**Use to** is only used when the word **did** is used before it: *It didn't use to matter; Did he use to play on the beach at Blackpool?*

## usual
Usual ends in **-ual**.

A related word is
  adverb **usually**

There are two **l**s in usually.

The word is made up of the *adjective* **usual** plus the *suffix* **-ly** added at the end. When the suffix **-ly** is added to a word which ends with **l**, there will be two **l**s:
  ***usual+ly = usually***

☆ Break these words down into smaller parts to help you remember the spellings:
  *u + su + al*
  *u + su + al + ly*

# V

## vaccinate
There are two **c**s and one **n** in vaccinate.

A related word is
*noun* **vaccination**

## vacuum
There is one **c** and two **u**s in vacuum.

## vague
Vague ends in **-gue**.

## vain, vein
These words sound the same and can be confused.

**Vain** means unsuccessful.
**Vain** also means proud of your looks or abilities.
**Veins** are the tubes in your body through which your blood flows.
A **vein** is also a mood or style:*writing in jocular vein.*

☆ Remember: V**ain** is **a**rrogant and a v**ein** is a **ve**ssel.

## valu**a**ble

There is an **a** in valuable which is sometimes missed out in speech. The ending is **-able**.

RULE A final silent **E** is dropped when an ending which begins with a vowel is added:

*value+able > valu+able = valuable*

## van**ill**a

There is one **n** and two **l**s in vanilla.

☆ Remember: **Vanill**a ice cream from the **van** made me **ill**.

## veg**e**table

There is an **e** after the **g** of vegetable which is often or missed out in speech.

☆ Remember that the word vegetable is connected to the word **vegetarian**, where the **e** is pronounced, and it may help you to remember that there is also an **e** after the **g** in veg**e**table.
☆ Or remember: **Get** ve**getable**s for the **table**.

## veg**e**tarian

The vowel after the **g** in vegetarian is **e**.

☆ Remember that **vege**tarians eat **vege**tables.

## ve**h**ement

There is a silent **h** in vehement. It begins with **veh-**.

The vowel which follows **veh-** is **e**.

A related word is
  noun **vehemence**

☆ Remember that ve**hem**ent contains the word **hem**.

## vehicle

There is a silent **h** in vehicle. It begins with **veh-**.

A related word is
  adjective **vehicular**

☆ Remember that ve**h**icle is connected to the adjective vehicular, where the **h** is pronounced, and it may help you to remember the **h** in ve**h**icle.

## vein, vain

These words sound the same and can be confused.

**Veins** are the tubes in your body through which your blood flows.
A **vein** is also a mood or style: writing in jocular vein.
**Vain** means unsuccessful.
**Vain** also means proud of your looks or abilities.

☆ Remember: V**a**in is **a**rrogant and a v**e**in is a v**e**ssel.

## vengeance
There is an **e** after the **g** in vengeance.

RULE A final silent **E** is usually dropped when an ending which begins with a vowel is added. But this **E** is retained for the endings -CE or -GE when these letters keep a *soft* sound:

*venge+ance = vengeance*

## verruca
There is one **s** and two **r**s in verruca.
The "oo" sound is spelt **u**.

## versatile
The vowel after **s** in versatile is **a**.

A related word is
*noun **versatility***

## veterinary surgeon
**Vet** is followed by -er in the word veterinary. This is often missed out in speech.
The ending is -**ary**.

☆ Remember: a **veter**an **veter**inary surgeon
☆ Or break the word veterinary down into smaller parts to help you remember the spelling:

*vet + er + in + ary*

## vigour
Vigour ends in -**our**.

A related word is
   adjective **vigorous**

There is no **u** before the **r** in vigorous.

RULE When the *adjective ending* **-ous** is added to a word ending in **-our**, the **u** of the **-our** is dropped:
   *vigour+ous > vigor + ous = vigorous*

RULE The "uss" sound at the end of an *adjective* is almost always spelt **-ous**.

*U.S. spelling*
   **vigor**

## villain
There are two **l**s in villain.
The ending is **-ain**.

## violence
There is an **o** after the **i** in violence. The beginning is **vio-**.

A related word is
   adjective **violent**

☆ Remember: **Vio**lations can be **vio**lent.

## viscount
There is a silent **s** before the **c** in viscount.

☆ Remember: A **viscount is count**ed an aristocrat.

## visible
Visible ends in **-ible**.

A related word is
  noun **visibility**

☆ Remember: You need two **i**s to make things vi**si**ble; you need four **i**s for extra vi**si**b**i**l**i**ty.

## visitor
Visitor ends in **-or**.

## volatile
The vowel after **l** in vol**a**tile is **a**.

A related word is
  noun **volatility**

## voluntary
There is an **a** after the **t** in volunt**a**ry which is sometimes missed out in speech. The ending is **-ary**.

## vulnerable
The vowel after **n** in vuln**e**rable is **e**.

☆ Remember: **Ner**ves can make you vul**ner**able.

**walnut**
There is only one **l** in walnut.

**wardrobe**
The ending of wardrobe is **-obe**.

☆ Remember that a ward**robe** is where you hang **robe**s.

**weather**
The vowel sound after **w** in weather is spelt **ea**. The beginning is **wea-**.

☆ Remember: What can you **wea**r for this **wea**ther?

**Wednesday**
The **n** in Wednesday comes straight after the **d**.

☆ Break this word down into smaller parts to help you remember the spelling:
*Wed + nes + day*

**weigh**
The "ay" sound in weigh is spelt **ei**.

There is a silent **gh** at the end.

Another related word is
   noun **weight**

☆ It may help you to remember that w**eight** and
h**eight** have the same spelling after the first letter.
☆ Or remember: He is **eight** stones in w**eight**.
☆ Or remember this word as being spelt **w** plus
the word **eight**:
   *w + eight = weight*

## w**ei**rd
The **e** comes before **i** in weird.

RULE Usually, **I** comes before **E** except after **c**
when they make the sound "ee".

However, **weird** is an <u>exception</u> to this rule, with
the **e** before the **i**.

☆ Remember: It is w**ei**rd how the **i** before **e** rule
is broken.

## wel̦come
There is only one **l** in welcome.

## whether
Whether begins with **wh-**.

The spelling of the word **weather**, the conditions

in the atmosphere, is sometimes confused with **whether**.

## which
Which begins with **wh-**.
There is no **t**, the ending is **-ich**.

The spelling of which is sometimes confused with **witch**, a woman with magic powers.

## whisky, whiskey
Both forms of this word begin with **wh-**.

**Whisky**, without an **e**, is **whisky** from Scotland.
**Whiskey**, with an **e**, is usually used for **whiskey** from Ireland, the United States, or Canada.

The *plural* of whisky is:
   **whiskies**

RULE The *plural* of a word which ends in a consonant plus **y** is made by changing the **y** to **i** and adding **-ES**:
   **whisky > whiski+es = whiskies**

The *plural* of whiskey is:
   **whiskeys**

RULE The *plural* of a word which ends in a vowel plus **y** is made by adding **s**:
   **whiskey+s = whiskeys**

## who's, whose

These words sound the same and they are often confused.

**Who's**, with an *apostrophe*, is a shortened form of **who is**: *He knows who's boss*; *Who's there?*
**Whose**, without an *apostrophe* and with an **e** at the end, is used when you are asking who something belongs to, or referring to something belonging or relating to things that have already been mentioned: *a little boy whose nose grew every time he told a lie*; *Whose coat is this?*

RULE In shortened forms of words or combinations of words with an *apostrophe*, the apostrophe appears in the place where a letter or letters have been missed out:

*who+is > who+s = who's*

## width

The ending of width is **-dth**.
There is no **e** in width, even though it is related to the word **wide**.

## wield

The **i** comes before the **e** in wield.

RULE I before E except after C, when they make the sound "ee".

## wife
The *plural* of wife is:
 *wives*

## withhold
There are two **h**s in withhold.

The word is made up of the words **with** and **hold**:
 *with+hold = withhold*

## wolf
The *plural* of wolf is:
 *wolves*

## wonderful
There is one **l** at the end of wonderful.

RULE · The *suffix* -**FUL** is always spelt with one **L**.

## wondrous
There is no **e** between the **d** and **r** in wondrous,
even though it is connected to the word **wonder**.
The ending is -**ous**.

RULE The "uss" sound at the end of an *adjective* is
almost always spelt -**OUS**.

## woollen
## woolly
There are two **l**s in woollen and woolly.

RULE When an ending which begins with a vowel is added to a word which ends in a vowel plus **L**, the final **L** is doubled:
*   **wool+en > wooll+en = woollen**
*   **wool+y > wooll+y = woolly**

*U.S. spellings*
    **woolen**
    **wooly**

Words related to woolly are
    *adjective* **woollier**
    *adjective* **woolliest**

RULE When any ending is added to a word that ends in a consonant plus **Y**, the **Y** is changed to **I** (unless the ending added already begins with **I**):
*   **woolly+er > woolli+er = woollier**
*   **woolly+est > woolli+est = woolliest**

## worship
Worship begins with **wor-**.

The different *verb* forms of worship are:
    **worships**
    **worshipped**
    **worshipping**

Another related word is
    *noun* **worshipper**

RULE When an ending which begins with a vowel is added to a word which ends in a single vowel plus a consonant, the consonant is doubled if the *stress* is on the end of the word.

The stress in worship is not on the end of the word, but the final consonant is still doubled:

**worship+ed > worshipp+ed = worshipped**
**worship+ing > worshipp+ing = worshipping**
**worship+er > worshipp+er = worshipper**

## wrack, rack

These two spellings can be confused.

**Wrack** or **rack** is an old word for destruction, but the form **rack** is more common: *rack and ruin*.
A **rack** is a framework for storing things.
A **rack** is also an old instrument of torture.
To **rack** is to cause suffering.
To **rack** is also to strain or shake violently: *a nerve-racking moment*.
You **rack** your brains when you try hard to think of something.

<u>wr</u>angle
<u>wr</u>ath
<u>wr</u>eck
<u>wr</u>estle
<u>wr</u>ench
<u>wr</u>inkle
<u>wr</u>ist

All the above words start with a silent **w**. They all begin with **wr-**.

## wrap

Wrap starts with a silent **w**. The beginning is **wr-**

The different *verb* forms of wrap are:
  **wraps**
  **wrapping**
  **wrapped**

Another related word is
  *noun* **wrapper**

RULE When an ending which begins with a vowel is added to a word which ends in a single vowel plus a consonant, the consonant is doubled if the *stress* is on the end of the word or if the word has only one part:

  **wrap+ing** > **wrapp+ing = wrapping**
  **wrap+ed** > **wrapp+ed = wrapped**
  **wrap+er** > **wrapp+er = wrapper**

## wreak

Wreak, meaning to cause (especially in wreak havoc) starts with a silent **w**. The beginning is **wr-** The "ee" sound is spelt **ea**.

## wring, ring

These two words sound the same and can be confused.

To **wring** something is to twist it.
A **ring** is the sound made by a bell.

A **ring** is also a circle or enclosure.

☆ Remember: You **w**ring out something **w**et.

## writhe
Writhe starts with a silent **w**. The beginning is **wr**.
There is an **e** at the end. The ending is **-the**.

## writing
Writing starts with a silent **w**. The beginning is **wr-**.
There is no **e** after the **t**.

RULE A final silent **E** is dropped when an ending which begins with a vowel is added:

*write+ing > writ+ing = writing*

## written
Written starts with a silent **w**. The beginning is **wr-**.
There is a double **t** in the middle.

## wry
Wry starts with a silent **w**. The beginning is **wr-**.

This spelling of wry, as in "a wry smile", is different from **rye**, a type of grass or grain.

# Y

## yacht
Yacht has **ach** in the middle.

## yield
The **i** comes before the **e** in yield.

RULE I before E except after C, when they make the sound "ee".

## yogurt _or_ yoghurt
Yogurt can be spelt with or without an **h** after the **g**.

Another much less common spelling is:
   *yoghourt*

## yoke, yolk
These two words sound the same and are often confused.

A **yoke** is an oppressive force or burden: *A country under the yoke of oppression.*
A **yoke** is also a wooden beam put across two animals so that they can be worked as a team.
To **yoke** things together is to link them: *They are*

*yoked to the fortunes of the Prime Minister.*
The yellow part of an egg is the **yolk**.

## your, you're
These two spellings are often confused.

**Your**, without an *apostrophe*, is used when you are referring to something belonging or relating to the person or people you are speaking to, or relating to people in general: *Your sister is right; Cigarettes can damage your health.*

**You're**, with an *apostrophe* and with an **e** at the end, is a shortened form of **you are**: *You're annoying.*

RULE In shortened forms of words or combinations of words with an *apostrophe*, the apostrophe appears in the place where a letter or letters have been missed out:

*you+are* > *you+re = you're*

## yours
There is no *apostrophe* in yours, although it indicates possession.

# Z

## zealous
This word is made up of the *noun* **zeal** plus the *suffix* **-ous** added at the end:

> *zeal+ous = zealous*

RULE The "uss" sound at the end of an *adjective* is almost always spelt **-ous**.

## zigzag
The different *verb* forms of zigzag are:

> *zigzags*
> *zigzagged*
> *zigzagging*

RULE When an ending which begins with a vowel is added to a word which ends in a single vowel plus a consonant, the consonant is doubled if the *stress* is on the end of the word:

> *zigzag+ed > zigzagg+ed = zigzagged*
> *zigzag+ing > zigzagg+ing = zigzagging*

## zoology
There is a double **o** at the start of zoology.

A related word is

*adjective* **zoological**

☆ Break these words down into two parts to help you remember the spellings:

***zoo + logy***
***zoo + logical***

Here are some of the terms used in this book and what they mean:

### accent
A mark placed above or below a letter which affects the way the letter is pronounced, for example **é**. These are usually found in words which have come into English from other languages.

### adjective
A word that adds to a description of a noun, for example, ***green*** *jersey*. Compare this with *adverb*, *noun*, and *verb*.

### adverb
A word that adds information about a verb or a following *adjective* or other *adverb*, for example *he walks **slowly**; it is **terribly** sad; he walks **very** slowly*. Compare this with *adjective*, *noun*, and *verb*.

### apostrophe
A punctuation mark (') that is used to show that one or more letters have been missed out of a word, as in *can't*. It is also used to show that something belongs to something else. There is a section on page 309 of this book which explains the apostrophe fully.

### consonant
A sound which you make by stopping the air flowing freely through your mouth; or a letter such as **p** or **m**, which stands for a sound like this. Compare this with *vowel*.

### hard
The sound of the letters **c** and **g** in words like *cat* or *give*, and not in words like *ceiling* or *gym*. Compare this with *soft*.

### noun
A word which refers to a person, thing, or idea, for example *John*, *table*, *tiredness*. Compare this with *adjective*, *adverb*, and *verb*.

### past tense
The form of a verb that is used to talk about things that happened before the present, for example **walked**, **ran**, **went**.

### plural
The form of a word that is used to refer to two or more people or things, for example *flowers*, *tomatoes*.

### prefix
A letter or group of letters added to the beginning of a word to make a new word, for example **<u>un</u>lucky**, **<u>pre</u>historic**, **<u>un</u>necessary**. Compare this with *suffix*.

*pronoun*
A word that is used to replace a noun, for example, **he**, **she**, **them**.

*soft*
The sound of the letters **c** and **g** in words like **ceiling** or **gym**, and not in words like **cat** or **give**. Compare this with *hard*.

*stress*
Emphasis on part of a word so that it sounds slightly louder, for example on **ve** in **de<u>ve</u>lop**.

*suffix*
A group of letters which is added to the end of a word to make a new word, for example **happi<u>ness</u>**, **faith<u>ful</u>**.

*verb*
A word that says what someone or something does or what happens to them, for example **be**, **become**, **take**, **run**. Compare this with *adjective*, *adverb*, and *noun*.

*vowel*
A sound made without your tongue touching the roof of your mouth or your teeth; or the letters **a**, **e**, **i**, **o**, and **u**, which stand for these sounds. Compare this with *consonant*.

Here are some basic spelling rules. If you recognize and remember these rules, it will help you to spell a difficult or unfamiliar word.

**1.a.** A final silent **E** is dropped when an ending which begins with a vowel is added, for example:

    ***accommodate+ion > accommodat+ion = accommodation***
    ***argue+able > argu+able = arguable***
    ***fascinate+ing > fascinat+ing = fascinating***

  **b.** This **E** is retained for the endings **-CE** or **-GE** when these letters keep a *soft* sound, for example:

    ***change+able = changeable***
    ***courage+ous = courageous***
    ***outrage+ous = outrageous***

**2.** When the adverb *suffix* **-LY** is added to an adjective which ends in a consonant followed by **-LE**, the **-LE** is usually dropped. For example:

    ***gentle+ly > gent+ly = gently***
    ***idle+ly > id+ly = idly***
    ***subtle+ly > subt+ly = subtly***

**3.** When an ending which begins with a vowel is added to a word which ends in a single vowel plus a consonant, the consonant is doubled if the stress is on the end of the word or if the word has only one part. For example:

> *admit+ance* > *admitt+ance* = *admittance*
> *begin+ing* > *beginn+ing* = *beginning*
> *equip+ed* > *equipp+ed* = *equipped*

**4.**   When an ending which begins with a vowel is added to a word which ends in a single vowel plus **L**, the **L** is doubled. For example:

> *cancel+ation* > *cancell+ation* = *cancellation*
> *excel+ent* > *excell+ent* = *excellent*
> *fulfil+ing* > *fulfill+ing* = *fulfilling*

**5.**   When an ending which begins with **E**, **I**, or **Y** is added to a word which ends in **C**, a **K** is also added to the **C** to keep its *hard* sound. For example:

> *picnic+ing* > *picnick+ing* = *picnicking*

An exception to this is **arc**, **arced**, **arcing**.

**6.**   When the *adjective suffix* **-OUS** or **-ARY** is added to a word which ends in **-OUR**, the **U** of the **-OUR** is dropped. For example:

> *glamour+ous* > *glamor+ous* = *glamorous*

*honour+ary > honor+ary =
honorary
humour+ous > humor+ous =
humorous*

7.  When an ending is added to a word which
    ends in a consonant plus **Y**, the **Y** changes
    to **I** (unless the ending added already begins
    with **I**). For example:
    *beauty+ful > beauti+ful = beautiful
    carry+age > carri+age = carriage
    woolly+er > woolli+er = woollier*

8.a.  The *plural* of a word which ends in a
    consonant plus **Y** is made by changing the
    **Y** to **I** and adding **-ES**, for example:
    *accessory > accessori+es =
    accessories
    memory > memori+es = memories
    whisky > whiski+es = whiskies*

  b.  The *plural* of a word which ends in a vowel
    plus **Y** is made by adding **s**, for example:
    *jersey+s = jerseys
    journey+s = journeys
    whiskey+s = whiskeys*

  c.  The *plural* of a word which ends in **s**, **x**,
    **z**, **sh**, or **ch** is made by adding **-es**,

for example:
> ***bus+es = buses***
> ***focus+es = focuses***

**d.** The *plural* of a word which ends in **-EAU** is made by adding **s** or **x**, for example:
> ***gateau+s = gateaus*** or
> ***gateau+x = gateaux***
> ***bureau+s = bureaus*** or
> ***bureau+x = bureaux***

**9.** When **AL-** is added as a *prefix* at the beginning of a word to make a new word, it is spelt with one **L**. For example:
> ***al+ready = already***
> ***al+though = although***
> ***al+together = altogether***

**10.** The suffix **-FUL** is always spelt with one **L**, for example:
> ***grateful***
> ***faithful***
> ***hopeful***

**11.** The "uss" sound at the end of an adjective is almost always spelt **-OUS**, for example:
> ***courageous***
> ***courteous***
> ***luscious***

**12.** I comes before **E** except after **c**, when they make the sound "ee". For example:

*fierce*
*niece*
*relieve*

but *ceiling*
*deceive*
*receive*

**13.a.** The name or names of an area on the map begin with a capital letter:

*Britain*
*Mediterranean*

**b.** The name of a religious group or its teachings begins with a capital letter:

*Buddhism*

These are the places where the apostrophe should be used:

1. In shortened forms of words or combinations of words, the apostrophe appears in the place where a letter or letters have been missed out:

   *do + not > do + nt = don't*
   *it + is > it + s = it's*
   *they + are > they + re = they're*

2.a. An apostrophe with the letter **s** is added to a *noun* or pronoun to indicate that something else which is mentioned belongs to or relates to it:

   *James's cat*
   *last week's news*

   b. An apostrophe alone is added to a *noun* that is already a *plural* <u>with</u> an **s**:

   *the winners' medals*
   *in three weeks' time*

   c. An apostrophe with the letter **s** is added to a *noun* that is already a *plural* <u>without</u> an **s**:

   *children's books*
   *men's clothes*

**d.** **It's** does not indicate "something that belongs to it". That is **its**, without an apostrophe. **It's** is the shortened form of **it is**.

**e.** The *pronouns* that already indicate that something is owned by or relates to them have no apostrophe:

> **hers**
> **ours**
> **theirs**
> **yours**

3. An apostrophe is not used to form a *plural* unless it is for a letter, number, or some other short word which rarely has another plural form:

> *Mind your p's and q's*
> *A row of 1's and a column of 2's*

The main differences in U.S. spellings are

1.  British words which end in **-OUR** are usually spelt **-OR** in the U.S.:
    *favor*
    *glamor*
    *rumor*

2.  British words which end in **-RE** are usually spelt **-ER** in the U.S.:
    *center*
    *liter*
    *theater*

3.a. British words which end in **-IZE** or **-ISE** are always spelt **-IZE** in the U.S.:
    *apologize*
    *emphasize*
    *recognize*

   b. Those which end in **-YSE** are spelt **-YZE**:
    *analyze*
    *breathalyze*

4.  Some words containing **AE** or **OE** in Britain always have **E** on its own in the U.S.:

*anesthetic*
*diarrhea*
*maneuver*

5. A final **L** is <u>not</u> doubled when an ending which begins with a vowel is added:
*canceled*
*jeweler*

**COLLINS GEM 1950s**

a mine of information

**COLLINS GEM 1960s**

a mine of information

**COLLINS GEM 1970s**
NO GAS

a mine of information

**COLLINS GEM 1980s**

a mine of information

**COLLINS Jane's CIVIL AIRCRAFT**

a mine of information

**COLLINS GEM CLANS & Tartans**

a mine of information

**COLLINS GEM Classic TV SERIES**

a mine of information

**COLLINS Jane's COMBAT AIRCRAFT**

a mine of information

**COLLINS GEM FIRSTS**

a mine of information

**COLLINS GEM GOLF**

a mine of information

**COLLINS GEM HILLWALKER'S Survival Guide**

a mine of information

**COLLINS GEM HOME EMERGENCY GUIDE**

a mine of information

**COLLINS GEM Collecting STAMPS**

a mine of information

**COLLINS GEM STARS**

a mine of information

**COLLINS GEM SUPERSTITIONS**

a mine of information

**COLLINS GEM Using Your SOFTWARE**

a mine of information